Making It Work:
A Handbook for Reading, Writing, Language, and Media

Marie Clayden
Dianne Fenner
Christine McAdam
Christine Straus

IRWIN PUBLISHING
Toronto, Canada

Copyright © 2003 by Irwin Publishing Ltd.

National Library of Canada Cataloguing in Publication Data

Main entry under title:

    Making it work: a handbook for reading, writing, language and media/Marie Clayden... [et al.].

Includes index.
ISBN 0-7725-2911-6

1. Readers (Secondary) 2. English language — Composition and exercises. I. Clayden, Marie

PE1408.M363 2002   428.6   C2002-901892-7

All rights reserved. It is illegal to reproduce any portion of this book in any form or by any means, electronic or mechanical, including photocopy, recording or any information storage and retrieval system now known or to be invented, without the prior written permission of the publisher, except by a reviewer who wishes to quote brief passages in connection with a review written for inclusion in a magazine, newspaper, or broadcast.

    Any request for photocopying, recording, taping, or for storing of informational and retrieval systems, of any part of this book should be directed in writing to CANCOPY (Canadian Reprography Collective), One Yonge Street, Suite 1900, Toronto, ON M5E 1E5.

Cover Design: Dave Murphy
Text Design: Alicia Countryman, Dave Murphy/ArtPlus Ltd.
Page Layout: ArtPlus Ltd.
Technical Art: ArtPlus Ltd
Project Management: Doug Panasis, Resources.too
Editorial Development: Susan Petersiel Berg
Photo Research and Permissions: Lisa Brant
Index: Liba Berry

Published by
Irwin Publishing Ltd.
325 Humber College Blvd.
Toronto, ON M9W 7C3

The authors and publisher would like to thank the following reviewers:

Ken Draayer, Niagara District School Board
Myra Junyk, Toronto District School Board
Diana Knight, Peel District School Board
Catherine Logan, Toronto District School Board
Carolyn Sheffield, Durham District School Board
Mary Lou Smitheram, Upper Canada District School Board
Catherine Stasiw, Toronto Catholic District School Board

We acknowledge for their financial support of our publishing program the Canada Council, the Ontario Arts Council, and the Government of Canada through the Book Publishing Industry Development Program (BPIDP).

See page 234 for a full list of acknowledgements.

Printed and bound in Canada

1 2 3 4   05 04 03 02

TABLE OF CONTENTS

How to Use this Handbook	iv

Literature Studies and Reading

What Are You Reading?	2
How to Use Reading Strategies to Understand Text	6
How to Summarize a Paragraph	13
How to Analyze Longer Prose Works	16
How to Understand and Analyze Poetry	20
How to Reflect on and Examine Individual Values	24
How to Understand Connotations of Words	27
How to Read Literature	30
How to Write a Character Sketch	37
How to Read Visual Information	42

Writing

The Writing Process	50
How to Research	54
How to Write a Paragraph	58
How to Write an Opinion Paper	62
How to Write a Report	67
How to Write a Formal Letter	70
How to Write a Résumé	76
How to Write a Covering Letter	83
How to Write and Send E-mail	89

Language

Using Language	94
How to Follow Oral Instructions	98
How to Identify the Main Idea while Listening	102
How to Create and Present an Oral Summary	105
How to Choose a Graphic Organizer to Summarize Discussion	110
How to Be an Effective Group Member	113
How to Complete Work in Groups	117
How to Create a Personal Dictionary	121
How to Build a Specialized Vocabulary	124
How to Create a Personal Style Guide	128
How to Choose Appropriate Language	132
How to Make a Presentation	136
How to Conduct an Interview	141

Media Studies

Media around You	146
How to Search on the Internet	150
How to Identify Elements of, and Create, a Magazine or Newspaper	154
How to Analyze and Create a Radio News Report	160
How to View a Television Program	165
How to Identify Bias	170
How to Analyze and Create Advertising	174
How to Create a Storyboard	180
How to Create a Video	184

Grammar

Parts of speech	190
Nouns	191
Pronouns	193
Verbs	196
Adjectives	197
Adverbs	199
Conjunctions and prepositions	201
Sentences	203
Sentence structures	203
Common sentence errors	205
Punctuation	207
Ending a sentence	207
Commas	209
Other punctuation	211
Connecting Words	216
Direct and indirect speech	219
Using Language	222
Synonyms	222
Antonyms	224
Homonyms	225
Spelling Rules	227
Index	229
Acknowledgements	234

How to Use this Handbook

Each unit of this handbook begins with an introduction to the main concepts of the unit. In each of the first four units, you will find a number of "how-to" entries that will help you attain the communications skills you need to succeed in school, in the workplace, and in the world around you.

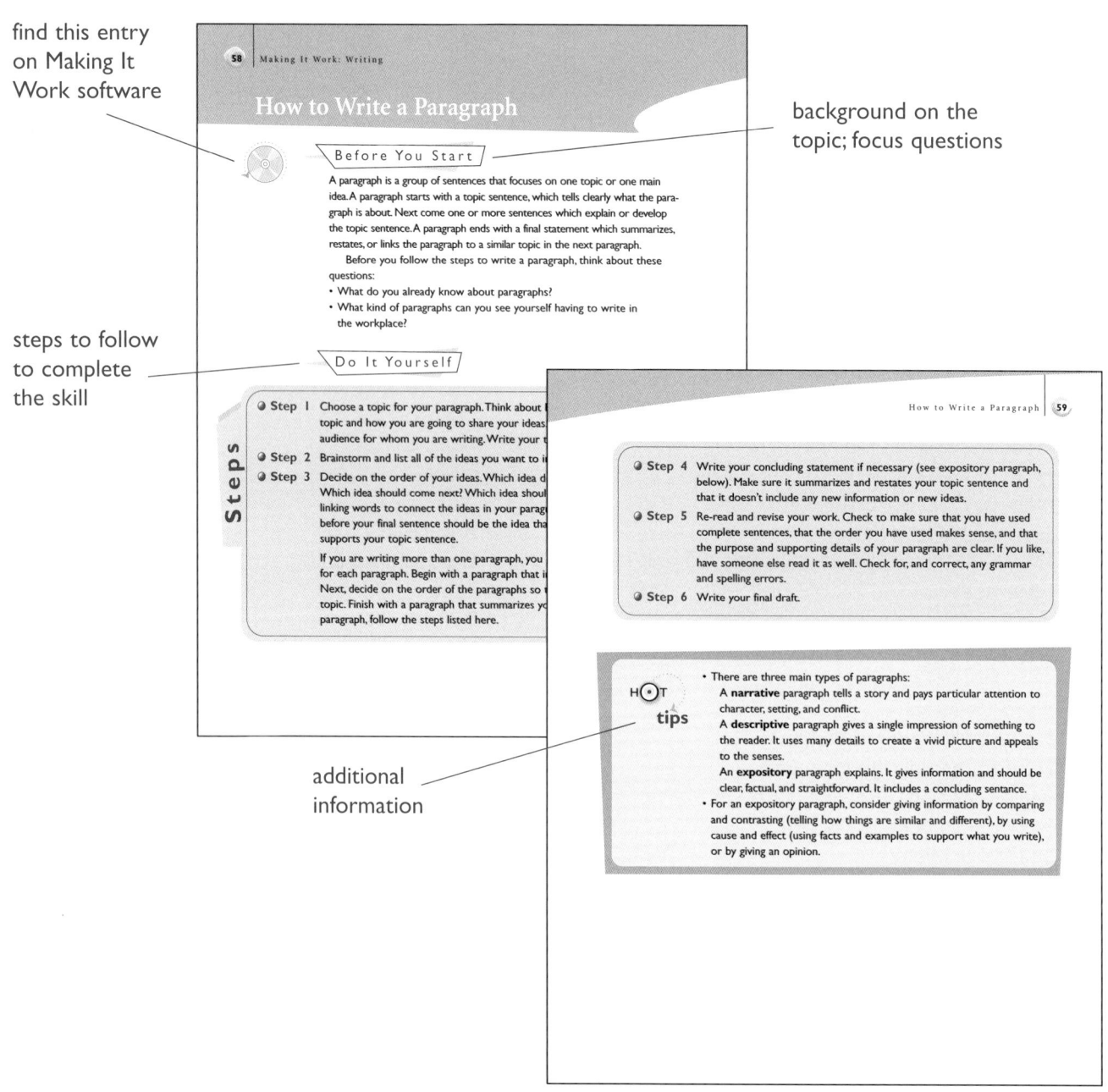

find this entry on Making It Work software

background on the topic; focus questions

steps to follow to complete the skill

additional information

How to Use this Handbook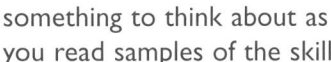

something to think about as
you read samples of the skill

Making It Work: Writing

Here is a model of each of the three kinds of paragraphs. As you read each model, think about the kind of information it gives you.

Model 1

Narrative Paragraph

topic sentence — The plan was about to be realized. Despite great difficulty acquiring parental approval, Sal, Josh, and Gerpet finalized their
supporting details — plans to begin the canoeing adventure they had been planning since they had first met and become close friends in Grade 9. Here they were — high-school graduates at last, 18 years old,
final statement — and ready to move on to the next phase of their lives, but not without completing the plan.

one or more samples
of the result of the skill;
notes identify elements
of the skill

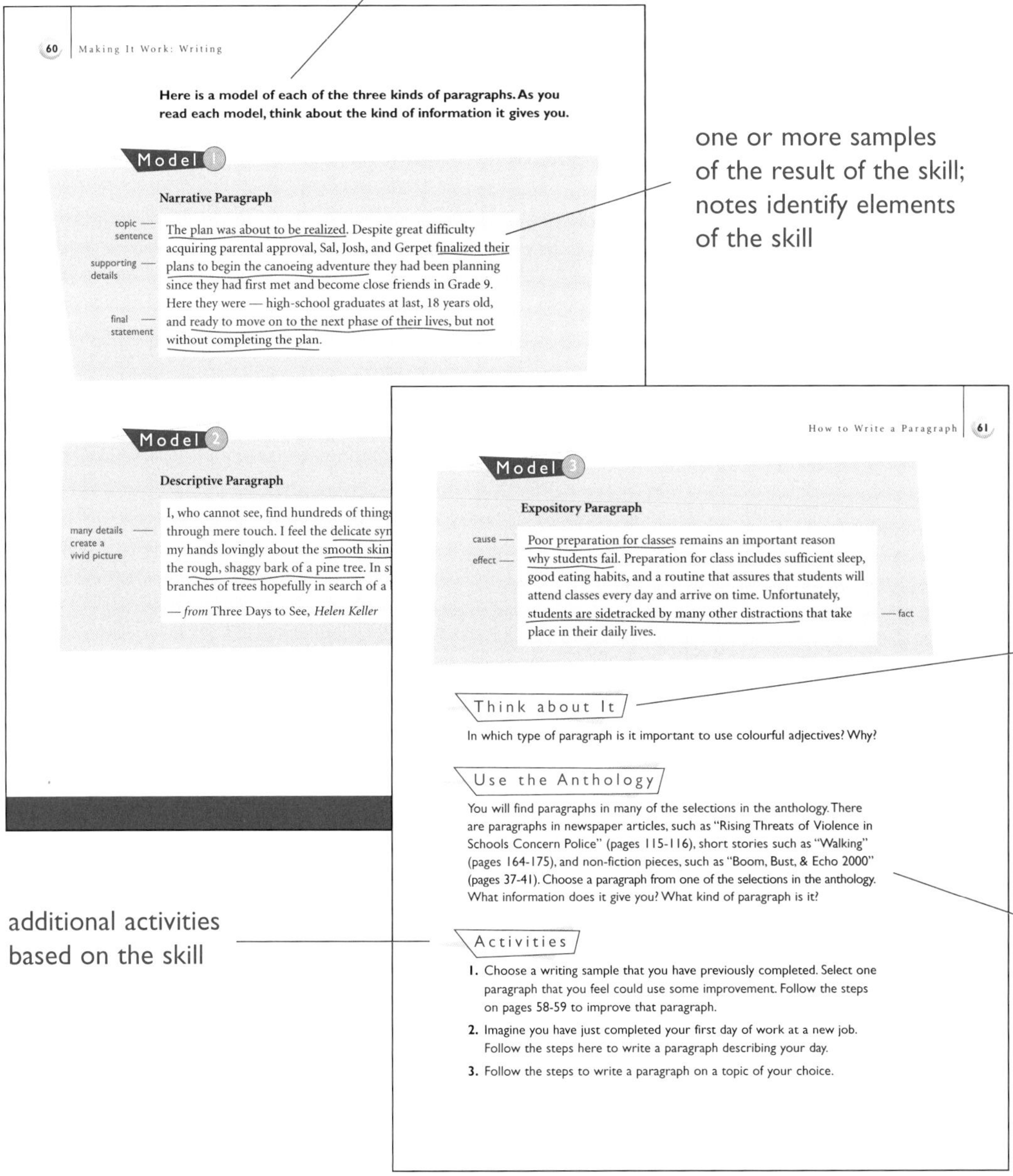

Model 2

Descriptive Paragraph

many details create a vivid picture — I, who cannot see, find hundreds of things through mere touch. I feel the delicate sy... my hands lovingly about the smooth skin the rough, shaggy bark of a pine tree. In s branches of trees hopefully in search of a

— from Three Days to See, Helen Keller

Model 3

Expository Paragraph

cause — Poor preparation for classes remains an important reason
effect — why students fail. Preparation for class includes sufficient sleep, good eating habits, and a routine that assures that students will attend classes every day and arrive on time. Unfortunately, students are sidetracked by many other distractions that take place in their daily lives. — fact

Think about It
In which type of paragraph is it important to use colourful adjectives? Why?

Use the Anthology
You will find paragraphs in many of the selections in the anthology. There are paragraphs in newspaper articles, such as "Rising Threats of Violence in Schools Concern Police" (pages 115-116), short stories such as "Walking" (pages 164-175), and non-fiction pieces, such as "Boom, Bust, & Echo 2000" (pages 37-41). Choose a paragraph from one of the selections in the anthology. What information does it give you? What kind of paragraph is it?

questions about
the models

ways to apply
the skill to
selections in
your anthology

Activities
1. Choose a writing sample that you have previously completed. Select one paragraph that you feel could use some improvement. Follow the steps on pages 58-59 to improve that paragraph.
2. Imagine you have just completed your first day of work at a new job. Follow the steps here to write a paragraph describing your day.
3. Follow the steps to write a paragraph on a topic of your choice.

additional activities
based on the skill

Literature Studies and Reading

TABLE OF CONTENTS

What Are You Reading?	2
How to Use Reading Strategies to Understand Text	6
How to Summarize a Paragraph	13
How to Analyze Longer Prose Works	16
How to Understand and Analyze Poetry	20
How to Reflect on and Examine Individual Values	24
How to Understand Connotations of Words	27
How to Read Literature	30
How to Write a Character Sketch	37
How to Read Visual Information	42

Making It Work: Literature Studies and Reading

What Are You Reading?

Look at the list below. Have you read any of these things lately?

television guides	baseball schedules	CD covers
music notes	timetables	e-mail messages
greeting cards	post cards	novels
magazines	short stories	poems
signs	comics	game instructions
instructional manuals	recipes	Internet sites
textbooks	job applications	classified ads
posters	phone messages	

Make a list in your notebook of all the different things you have read in the past week. What made you want to read each one? What information did you get from each?

The upcoming section of your handbook will give you lots of strategies to help you when you read — no matter what you read.

▶ Why read?

People read for all kinds of reasons: for enjoyment, for information, for instructions. Reading fiction — poems, stories, novels, plays, and screenplays — can take you into other worlds. Reading non-fiction gives you information. Both kinds of reading can help you to see the world in a different way. Reading helps you:

- increase your knowledge
- gather information to support an opinion or to compare differing ideas
- add to your understanding by finding supporting details
- find how to do something (use the Internet, write a report, play a game)

- directly use text to answer a question
- locate the main idea in a section, chapter, story, newspaper article, or poem
- understand an author's purpose and respond in a personal way to text.

▶ Understanding what you read

A good reader knows that the purpose of reading is to understand — to make sense of the text. Good readers use what they know about the sounds of English to understand words and groups of words. They use what they know about how texts are organized to locate information and ideas. They use their own knowledge and experiences to understand what they are reading. And they interpret other kinds of visual information to add meaning to what they are reading.

▶ Building understanding in reading

Recognizing what words mean

Skill	Strategy
Recognizing words	Divide complex words into parts: find the root or base words and add the meaning of the affixes (parts that come before and after the word). un + assist + ed prefix root suffix
Understanding words	Predict and confirm what words mean in the sentence in which they are used.

Understanding directly-stated information

Skill	Strategy
Answer a question asking for information in the text.	Look for key words from the question in the text.
Locate the main idea.	Use the title as a clue. read the first and/or last sentences of the paragraph.
Find evidence that supports the main idea.	Highlight key words and phrases.
Recognize the organization of ideas and details.	Locate key words and phrases that signal order, compare/contrast, cause/effect.

Understanding indirectly-stated information

Skill	Strategy
Making inferences or "reading between the line"	Predict what will happen. Use clues to make reasoned guesses about what the author means.
Interpreting ideas or information	Find directly-stated information, and think about its meaning and importance.
Interpreting mood and tone	Consider your feelings as you read the text. Examine the words that cause a reaction and create a mood.

Interpreting

Skill	Strategy
Connect the text to your own life and experiences.	Ask: what does this situation remind me of in my own life?
Compare the text to your own knowledge and understanding.	Ask and explain: What would I have done differently? How would someone I know solve this? Is the theme true based on what I know? Do I agree with the author? How has the text changed my point of view? How does my perspective compare to the author's?
Compare the text to others you've read.	Think of another text that presents the same situation or idea. How do they compare? Which one is more effective? More relevant? Do you believe to be true?

How to Use Reading Strategies to Understand Text

Before You Start

To read different kinds of texts, you need to know different reading strategies. Some strategies are useful for understanding what you read. Other strategies are useful for remembering what you read.

Before you follow the steps to use different reading strategies, think about the following questions:
- What do you do now to help you understand what you read?
- What do you do now to help you remember what you read?

Do It Yourself

Before, During, and After Reading

Steps

- **Step 1** Choose something to read, or read something that you have been assigned. As you follow the steps, make notes in your reading response journal of your answers to the questions.

- **Step 2** Before reading, ask yourself these questions:

    What kind of text is this?
    Why am I reading this?
    What do I already know about this topic?
    How is this text organized?
    What information can I find in any headings?
    What information can I find in any diagrams or illustrations?
    What word meanings do I need to check?

- **Step 3** During reading, ask yourself:

    What will happen next?
    What are the key words that catch my attention?

What main idea do the key words highlight?
What am I learning about this topic as I read?

- **Step 4** After reading, ask yourself:

  What did I learn?
  What new information did I find?
  What new words did I learn that are specific to this topic?

- **Step 5** Read over the notes you have made. Have you answered all of the questions about the reading? Is there anything that is still unclear? Read the piece again to complete your notes.

Do It Yourself

Consider How the Text is Organized

- **Step 1** Choose an informational text to read, or read one that you have been assigned. You might look at a chapter of a Science or History book, or a non-fiction selection from the anthology.

- **Step 2** Examine the structure of the text you are reading, and look for the elements listed below. A chapter of a Science book may have all of these elements; a non-fiction article may only have some of them.

  main heading — tells you the topic or subject of the text

  introductory paragraph — introduces the topic, gives definitions and background

  subheadings — break up the larger topic into smaller ones. The subheading identifies the subject or topic that will be explained in the paragraphs.

  concluding paragraph — summarizes the main ideas

  diagrams, figures, charts, graphs — represent important ideas, facts, and details in a visual way

> **design features of print** — bold or italic print usually shows a key word that is identified somewhere else in the text (such as in a glossary) or emphasizes an important fact or idea
>
> - **Step 3** Read the main heading and the subheadings to get an overall impression of what the text will be about.
> - **Step 4** Find the bold or italicized words and find their meanings.
> - **Step 5** Read the introduction.
> - **Step 6** Read the rest of the text, using a visual or graphic organizer to record key ideas.

Do It Yourself

Remembering What You Read: An Aloud Strategy

- **Step 1** Choose a paragraph to read or read one that is assigned to you.
- **Step 2** As you read, note the topic and the important details, either with self-stick notes or, if you are reading a photocopy, with a highlighter marker.
- **Step 3** Cover the paragraph so that you can't see it. Aloud, say to yourself the information that you have read. Say the topic of the paragraph and the important details in your own words.
- **Step 4** Check the paragraph again to see if you remembered all the information.

Do It Yourself

Remembering What You Read: Using Study Cards

- **Step 1** Choose a section of informational text that you might have to study for an upcoming test.

- **Step 2** Create study cards by recording notes about key ideas and details on index cards. Read the first subtitle and the paragraphs that follow. On separate cards, write the names of all people, places, and important numbers or terms, facts, and details that appear in the paragraphs. Repeat Step 2 until you have a complete set of study cards for each important detail in the text.

- **Step 3** When you have found most or all of the key ideas or details, read each one. Take notes about the information that each one gives you. Reading your notes will give you an idea of what the text is about.

- **Step 4** Read the subtitle again (for example, Types of Engines for Trucks). Turn it into a test question (for example, What are the types of engines for trucks?). Write the question on an index card. On the other side of the card, write the answer.

- **Step 5** Repeat the note-taking part of Step 3 to create a set of study cards that contain all the main ideas and sample test questions.

- **Step 6** Read each card that you have made. Explain each detail and what it tells about the topic. Try to answer the questions on the card without looking at the answers.

10 | Making It Work: Literature Studies and Reading

- Think of your purpose for reading (studying, enjoyment, finding the main idea) before choosing a reading strategy.
- Try different strategies for the same piece of text to see which one works best for you.
- Keep interacting with the text while you read — recall details, make predictions, recap ideas, find key words, and draw conclusions.

Here are some texts. Think about which strategy would be most useful for understanding each text.

Model 1

introductory statement — Canada's transportation network is extremely important to the country's economy. Raw materials from mines, forests, fisheries, and farms are transported to processing plants, and manufactured goods are <u>transported</u> to markets in Canada and elsewhere. People use the many means of transportation to crisscross the country visiting, vacationing, and doing business.

key word —

new information — Canada's transportation network performs another, perhaps less obvious, task. It links all of Canada's diverse regions, making people feel that they belong to one, unified country.

UNIT 2: *Electric Circuits*

3.1 Learning about Electricity

Electricity is a form of energy. It is produced by the movement of electrons. But do you know what actually happens when you flip a switch to turn on the light, or the computer, or the television set? Why don't all the lights go out in your house when one light bulb burns out? Electricity is very useful, but if people do the wrong thing, electricity can also hurt. In some cases it can even kill. Safety is key when it comes to electricity.

Electric Circuits

How does electricity flow? Electricity flows through paths, or **electric circuits**. Electrons travel through these paths, but only if they can move around the path and get back to where they started. If the path is broken, the electrons will not move.

A **closed circuit** allows electrons to travel through an unbroken path and back to where they started. An **open circuit** has a break in the path. Electrons will not move through an open circuit.

All circuits must contain three things: connecting conductors, an energy source, and a load. A **conductor** is a device, such as a wire, that allows electricity to pass easily through it. An **energy source**, such as a battery, is what gives the circuit its energy. A **load** is a device or appliance that uses the energy, such as a light bulb.

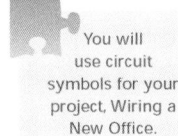
You will use circuit symbols for your project, Wiring a New Office.

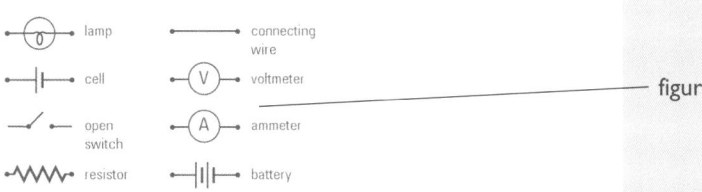

FIGURE 3.2 These are the symbols for the basic parts of a circuit.

Think about It

What information would you include on your study cards if you were studying the text in Model 2? What other reading strategy could you use for Model 2? Why?

Use the Anthology

Choose a piece of non-fiction from the anthology. Use a graphic organizer (see How to Choose a Graphic Organizer to Summarize Discussion, pages 110-112) and the steps here to make notes about it. If you like, do the same for a piece of fiction from the anthology. Did you choose a different organizer? Why?

Activities

1. Read the assigned chapter from your textbook in another course and use a graphic organizer to make notes about what you have read.

2. Read a newspaper or magazine article about a job or a workplace that interests you. Choose one of the reading strategies in this entry to find out more about the job or the workplace. Summarize your findings. Was the reading strategy you chose useful? Explain.

How to Summarize a Paragraph

Before You Start

Many types of informational and literary texts present their ideas in paragraphs. Think of paragraphs as the building blocks of texts. In informational text, each paragraph develops one main idea or topic. It has a topic sentence, sentences with details that support and describe or develop the topic, and a concluding or closing sentence. By presenting ideas in paragraphs, the writer gives the reader the chance to think about each key idea one at a time so the reader can build understanding in a longer piece of text.

Before you follow these steps to summarize a paragraph, think about these questions:
- Where do you usually find the main idea in a paragraph?
- What do you read (magazines, newspapers, articles)? What kind of information are you looking for?

Do It Yourself

Steps

- **Step 1** Look at a piece of writing your teacher asks you to read, or choose one yourself from the anthology, a newspaper, or a magazine. Read the first paragraph of the selection.
- **Step 2** Re-read the paragraph. Find the main idea, usually in the first sentence. Highlight key details in the paragraph.
- **Step 3** Make point-form notes of the main idea, the details that follow, and the concluding sentence of each paragraph.
- **Step 4** Using your point-form notes, write a sentence to express the main idea of the paragraph in your own words.
- **Step 5** Write one or two sentences in your own words that tell the detail and/or facts of the paragraph.
- **Step 6** Write a sentence to express the closing thought of the paragraph, in your own words. By finishing Steps 4, 5, and 6, you have summarized the paragraph.

14 Making It Work: Literature Studies and Reading

HOT tips
- The main idea of a paragraph is often in the topic or first sentence.
- The title can help you identify the main idea.
- Facts and details help you understand the main idea more completely.
- The concluding sentence restates the main idea.

Here are two pieces of informational text. What is different about the way each one is organized?

Model 1

the main idea is usually in the headline

A teen's 'twisted' cry for help: Fictional story about avenging the bullies who tormented him lands 16-year-old in jail

By Aaron Sands, *Ottawa Citizen*

the first few paragraphs include key details, answer Who, What, When, Where, Why, How

CRYSLER — It was a creative writing assignment for his favourite class, to be read aloud as a dramatic monologue.

It became a tormented 15-year-old boy's way of pleading with the bullies to stop the cruelty.

His story resulted in the police storming his family's home in this village east of Ottawa, arresting him, strip-searching him and locking him away in a youth detention centre.

The boy, who cannot be identified under provisions of the Young Offenders Act, is charged with uttering death threats — the threat of an unnamed character to bomb an unnamed school in a fictional story.

OPP spent two weeks investigating allegations that the boy, who was 15 at the time, had threatened students at Tagwi Secondary, a high school of 500 students in Avonmore, about 20 kilometres northwest of Cornwall.

He remains in custody today, a month later, because of his work of fiction. He spent his 16th birthday, Christmas and New Year's alone and in jail.

a photograph gives information

Teen with police officer

a caption with the photograph gives information

Model 2

the main idea is usually in the topic sentence

The destruction of the Wall began in the early evening of Thursday, November 9 [1989], soon after the first wave of East Berliners…burst upon the West. One…young man with a knapsack on his back somehow hoisted himself up on the Wall directly across from the Brandenburg Gate. He sauntered along the top of it, swinging his arms casually at his sides…a new generation of border guards took aim at a new kind of target and fired — but only with power hoses and without much conviction. The conqueror of the Wall continued his promenade, soaked to the skin, until at last the guards gave up. Then he lowered his knapsack and poured the water toward the East, in a gesture that seemed to say, "Goodbye to all that."

supporting details appear in the rest of the paragraph

supporting details answer the questions Who, What, When, Where, Why, How

a concluding sentence summarizes the details of the paragraph

— from "The Berlin Wall Crashes Down" by Robert Darnton

Think about It

How are the paragraphs in the two models similar? Different? Why do you think this is so?

Use the Anthology

Choose one paragraph from each of three different non-fiction texts in the anthology (for example, a newspaper article, a magazine article, an expository text, an essay). Compare and contrast how each paragraph is organized.

Activities

1. Find an article, that includes a photograph, from this week's newspaper. State where you found the piece and record its main idea. Read the first few paragraphs, and list all of the supporting details, that relate to the main idea (who, what, when, where, why, and how).

2. Look at the photograph that accompanies the article you chose. How does it add to your understanding of the news article? List the details in the caption that support your answer.

3. Write a paragraph summarizing the news article you chose. Follow the steps on page 13.

How to Analyze Longer Prose Works

Before You Start

Prose uses paragraphs to express its ideas. (Poetry uses stanzas or poetic lines, and plays use scripts with dialogue and stage directions.) Because prose uses paragraphs as its building blocks, you can use what you know about paragraphs to understand longer prose works.

Do It Yourself

Steps

- **Step 1** Choose a longer prose piece or use one that your teacher gives you to read. Skim it to figure out what kind of text it is, and use any features of the text to get a sense of the topic.

- **Step 2** After your first reading, make notes to answer the following questions:

    What do you think is the purpose of the work? Why?
    Who is the intended audience?
    What feelings did you have as you read it?
    What is the style like? Is it simple or complex? Is the tone serious or funny?
    How does the style help the writer share his or her message?

- **Step 3** Begin writing a prose analysis to solidify your thoughts. A prose analysis is a critical evaluation in three or four paragraphs. To write a prose analysis, follow the steps below. You might consider writing a paragraph for each group of questions.

    1. Note your first impressions:
        What is your overall impression of this text?
        What did you like about it?
        What did you dislike?
        What was challenging about it?
        What questions do you have?

How to Analyze Longer Prose Works

2. Analyze the context:
   Who wrote the work?
   What biases does the author have (see How to Identify Bias, pages 170-173)?
   What is the author's point of view?
   When was it written? Is it current or out–of–date?
   For what audience is it written? Are you part of that audience?

3. What effect did this text have on you? Why?

4. Explain how the text:
   — appeals to reason (What arguments are given? What are the author's conclusions? What reasons support the conclusions? How convincing is the author?)
   — appeals to emotions (What value and emotion words does the author use? What is convincing about the language the author uses?)

5. Would you recommend this text to another reader? Why or why not?

Step 4 Complete a draft of your prose analysis. Read it to, or share it with, a partner, and revise it so the ideas are clear and complete. Then edit it for grammar, spelling, punctuation, and language usage.

- To identify the writer's tone, try to "hear" the writer. Listen to the writer's tone of voice as if he or she were reading the text to you.
- You don't have to answer every question in the Do It Yourself section. Choose the prompts that fit the text and what you want to say about it.

This model begins with part of a longer prose work and is followed by a prose analysis. What do you expect to learn from the analysis?

Model

My Cycling Life

by Steve Bauer

… I've won my share of major events, and those experiences are wonderful motivators to keep me pushing for more success. Another method I use to elevate my overall level of performance is to pursue specific goals within a race. One of my goals had always been to wear the Yellow Jersey, symbolic of the leading rider in the Tour de France. But the highlight of the 1988 Tour for me was getting the Yellow Jersey back after I'd won it in the first stage. Winning it the first time was a big bonus, something that had eluded me for four years. But getting it back after one week was something really special.

…Wearing the Yellow Jersey means you're not just part of the race, you're the focus of the race. Everyone's attention is on you. This is the biggest, most publicized cycling event in the world, and here you are with the Jersey that shows you're number one so far along the road. It's an honour and you feel a responsibility to do your absolute best to defend it, which is harder than ever to do because you know that you're in the limelight and everyone is out to catch you. But it gives you an extra surge of energy, a psychological boost that helps you perform at your best. It gave me the determination to give my best performance ever and helped me finish fourth overall in the Tour in 1988.

They say that the Yellow Jersey gives you wings, and it certainly makes for a powerful feeling. But similar rewards and pleasures are there for any cyclist. All you have to do is to pedal your bike.

Prose Analysis of *My Cycling Life*

When I read this article by Steve Bauer, my first impression was that it takes a lot of hard work and dedication to be a top athlete, especially a top cyclist. I'm glad that he described what it was like to race when you're wearing the Yellow Jersey: he was very honest. I wish that he'd told me more about being in the race, especially trying to get around other cyclists who are in front of you. I'd like to hear more stories about bike racing. One of the things that I think is very true in what he said was that you really have to want to win and make that your goal. I'd like to know if that strategy is harder in some races than in others!

I don't know much about Steve Bauer, but I know from his article that he loves cycling. He sounds like the kind of person who would be great to listen to, to help us reach higher and be more than we are. The article is old, so I wonder if he really is our top cyclist now.

The effect the article had on me was to help me see myself as a winner. I'm a swimmer, but I sometimes don't believe that I can win. I'm going to try to see myself ahead of the others next time, and see if that makes a difference. I would definitely recommend this article to anyone who knows they can do it, and just needs a bit more confidence.

Annotations:
- reader's first impression
- what the reader liked
- what the reader would like more information about
- point of view of author
- how current the information is
- the effect of the text on the reader
- recommendation to others

Think about It

Were your predictions about the prose analysis correct? Did it offer all the information you wanted? Explain.

Use the Anthology

Read "Alone on the Ocean" (page 111). What is the purpose of this work? Who is the intended audience? What is your impression of this piece?

Activities

1. Select a prose piece from a magazine and one from a newspaper. Write a prose analysis of each one.

2. Select a short story or read one assigned by your teacher. Write a prose analysis of it.

How to Understand and Analyze Poetry

Before You Start

A poem is a composition in verse form. Unlike prose writers, who use paragraphs to express ideas, poets express ideas in stanzas, or verses, or in poetic lines. There are many different types of poems. Some poems rhyme, while others don't.

A poem is different from other forms of writing because of the way the words work together to create sounds, images, and rhythm. The arrangement of words creates a kind of music that makes poetry very different from prose.

The language of poetry is also found in many of your favourite songs, because poetry and music are linked.

Before you follow the steps to analyze poetry, think about the following:

- What is your favourite poem or song? What do you like about the words in the poem or song?
- What poem have you read recently? What was it about? How did the words help get the meaning across?

Do It Yourself

Step 1 Choose a poem to read, or read one that your teacher assigns. Before you read, scan the poem for vocabulary. List several words that are new or that interest you. What do these words tell you about the topic of the poem?

Step 2 Make notes for a poetry analysis using the following outline.

Personal Response
Did you like or dislike this poem? Explain your choice.

Content
What is happening in the poem?
If the poem tells a story, retell the events in order.

If the poem doesn't tell a story, list the sequence of thoughts in the poem.
Who is the speaker?
What is the occasion or the setting?

Purpose
What did you hear/see/feel by reading the poem?
Why do you think the poet wrote this poem?
What do you think the poet wanted you to feel, see, or know? How do you know?

Tone
If you could imagine the poet reading this poem to you, how would you describe the poet's tone of voice?

Word Usage
Select five words from the poem that stand out. Why do these words stand out?
What pictures/feelings/sounds are created by these words?

Poetic Devices
Here are some examples of poetic devices:
- similes, metaphors, and personification are all types of comparisons that create images, or pictures:
  - a simile compares two things using "like" or "as" (Her face was like a just-opened flower.)
  - a metaphor is a more direct comparison that says that two unlike things are the same (Her face was a wall turned blankly toward him.)
  - personification gives human qualities to non-human things (The cathedral stands knee-deep in the town.)
- Alliteration is the repetition of initial consonants (The bird's fire-fangled feathers dangle down.)
- A symbol is a concrete object which suggests a more complex, abstract idea (roses represent love, a dove represents peace).

What images and symbols do you see in the poem? What effect do they have on you?
What sound devices does the poet use? What effect do they have on you?

Making It Work: Literature Studies and Reading

- **Step 3** Examine your notes. Share your findings with a partner. Add any missing details and clarify anything that is confusing.
- **Step 4** Write a draft of your analysis. Write a separate paragraph for each of the topics in your outline. Revise and edit your draft.

Hot tips

- A word is more than just letters joined together. It has a sound, it has a dictionary meaning, and it has an emotional meaning (see How to Understand Connotations of Words, page 27). Think about all three aspects of key words in a poem.

This model begins with a poem and is followed by a poetry analysis. Read the title of the poem. What do you think the poem will be about?

Model

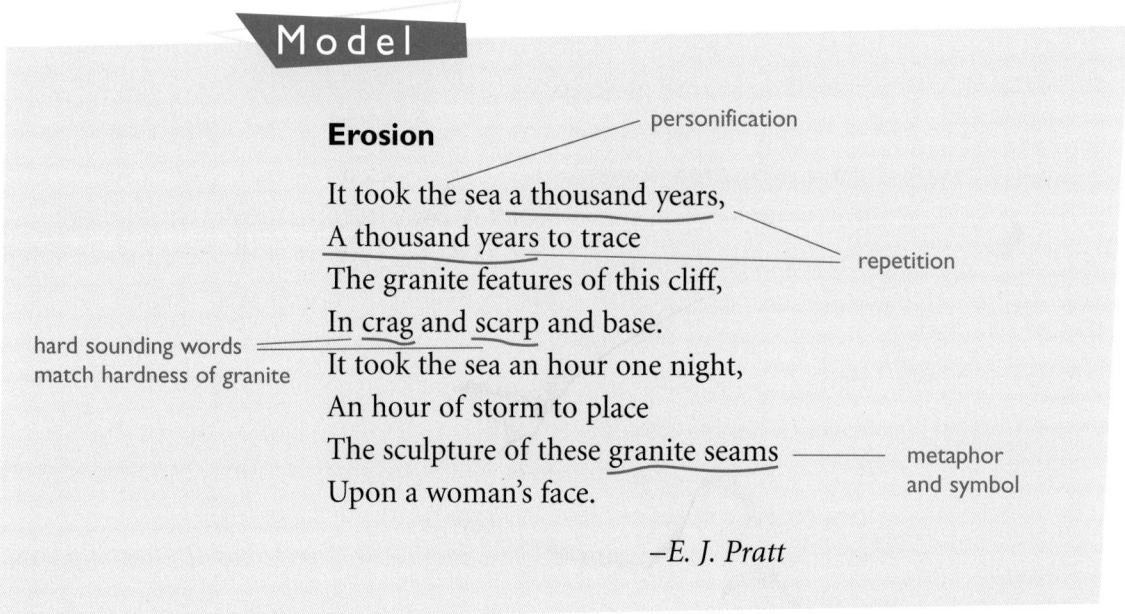

Erosion — personification

It took the sea a thousand years,
A thousand years to trace — repetition
The granite features of this cliff,
In crag and scarp and base.
It took the sea an hour one night,
An hour of storm to place
The sculpture of these granite seams — metaphor and symbol
Upon a woman's face.

—E. J. Pratt

hard sounding words match hardness of granite

How to Understand and Analyze Poetry | 23

Model

Poetry analysis

personal response — I liked the poem *Erosion* by E. J. Pratt because it contrasts the power of nature in two short stanzas. Pratt creates a vivid image of the sea by the use of poetic devices and unusual vocabulary.

The poem tells how powerful the sea can be: it can both create an unusual landscape and take the life of a person. — *what the poem is about*

Pratt gives human characteristics to the sea when he writes, "it took the sea a thousand years/to trace the granite features of this cliff" and "An hour of storm to place the sculpture of these granite seams." This personification creates an eerie feeling because the poet wants us to see the sea both as a power of nature and as an almost human master of the fate of the woman's loved one. — *poetic devices the poet used* / *what poet wants reader to see*

The use of the hard sounding words, "crag and scarp and base" match the hardness of granite. — *words that stand out, and why*

The final effect that the poem has on this reader is that it shows how with very simple language a skilled poet can convey strong emotion and draw a sharp picture of contrast from the commonplace. — *effect of poem on reader*

Think about It

What are "granite seams / Upon a woman's face"? What has happened to place these seams on the woman's face? What is the effect of the repetition in the poem?

Use the Anthology

Read "I Can't Write No Pretty Poem" (pages 47-49). What do you think of Geraldine's poem? Why do you think writing poetry may be a challenge?

Activity

1. Listen to your favourite song. What does it mean to you? Write down the words and complete a poetry analysis using the guidelines here. Did you find any new meaning?

How to Reflect on and Examine Individual Values

Before You Start

The themes and conflicts that we read about in fiction can be a lot like the ones in our own lives. A good way to understand text is to step away from it and think about what it means to you. You can also think about how you feel about the meaning of the values or ideas in the text. Knowing and evaluating how you feel about issues can help you set goals for learning in life, in school, and in the workplace.

Before you follow these steps to reflecting on and examining your own values, think about these questions:

- What do you think of as your own values? Do you usually act according to those values?
- What situations have you been in that challenge your values? How do you react to situations like that?

Do It Yourself

Steps

- **Step 1** Choose a piece of fiction to read, or read one that is assigned to you. Before you read, look at the title and determine what you think the text will be about. Create a set of questions that you want the text to answer.

- **Step 2** Read the text to the point at which you recognize the conflict and some of its key components.

- **Step 3** Think about the main conflict in the piece of fiction. Write notes to summarize that conflict. What is the conflict? What led to the conflict? Who is involved in the conflict?

- **Step 4** Ask yourself some questions to help you think about your own reaction to the conflict. Your questions might include:
  – What would I do in this situation?
  – What would be a good solution?
  – How would I put the solution in place?

How to Reflect on and Examine Individual Values

- **Step 5** Finish reading the story. Reflect on it, and describe how the conflict was resolved. Would you have handled the conflict the same way? Explain why or why not.

- **Step 6** Reflect on the values of the main character: How did his or her values influence the outcome of the conflict? Reflect on your own values: How would your values affect the outcome of the story? Explain how your values are similar to, or different from, those of the main character.

- When reflecting about what you might do in a similar situation to the one in a story, think about the values and principles that are important to you. How do these influence the way you think and act?

The following is an example of a conflict that you might face. How would you handle the conflict?

Model 1

Your grandmother has had a stroke and must leave her apartment to live with your family. She is bringing her two cats with her. Your parents have asked you to share a room with your younger sister so that your grandmother can have your bedroom. You don't get along with your sister.

— situation

— a decision you will have to make

Model 2

Your parents want you to go to college. You want to go to an accredited program for massage therapy.

— situation

— decision and negotiations to make

Think about It

What would you do in each one of these situations? Have you ever been affected by a similar situation? How did you react?

Use the Anthology

Read the story "Walking" (pages 164-175). Follow the steps on pages 24-25 of the Handbook to reflect on and examine your own values and how they compare with those you see in the story.

Activities

1. Write a response to two of the three following situations. If you were this person, how would you feel, and what would you do?

   - Your parents are always comparing you to your older sister who is an exemplary role model. She was nominated Junior Citizen of the year and has been awarded a scholarship to university. You try your best at school but it seems like everything is a struggle. Your parents just think you have to work harder.
   - Your family reunion is to be held during March Break. Everyone is excited about seeing you. Family members often refer to you as the "one who will succeed." But you have been invited to go skiing with your friends during March Break.
   - Your best friend is getting into serious trouble at school and in the community because of the influence of some new friends.

2. Examine your responses to each situation. Write a short piece about yourself, in paragraph form, to answer the questions that follow.

   - What did you learn about your values as you placed yourself in these situations?
   - Do you think that most others would feel and act as you would in these situations? Why or why not?
   - Think of a conflict that you've had recently. Describe it, and explain how you dealt with it. How did your values help to guide you to a solution?

How to Understand Connotations of Words

Before You Start

All words have a literal, or dictionary meaning, called a denotative meaning. Many words and phrases also have an emotional meaning, or connotation, also called a connotative meaning. The connotation of a word is the way the word makes you feel, or the image it makes you see. Where would you prefer to eat lunch — at a fast-food place, a diner, a greasy spoon, or a restaurant? Each is a place to eat, but the words used to describe the place give the reader a different understanding of that place. A word's connotation depends on your own experiences and values.

Before you follow the steps to understand connotation, think about these questions:
- What words would you use to describe yourself?
- What words would you use to describe your closest friend?
- If you chose different words, how would they change the impression that someone gets of you or your friend?

Do It Yourself

Steps

- **Step 1** Choose a selection to read, or read one assigned by your teacher, that describes a person, place, or thing.
- **Step 2** Read the selection once. Then read it a second time, this time locating and listing all of the words that create a strong impression of the subject of the text.
- **Step 3** Consider carefully the words you have listed. Group them in the categories below. Decide if the word is:

neutral	positive	negative
good	bad	powerful
weak	beautiful	ugly

- **Step 4** Write your answers to Step 3. Explain why connotations are important.

Making It Work: Literature Studies and Reading

- When you read a text that you react to strongly, list the words that stand out in your mind. Think about their connotations and how they might have helped to get a strong reaction from you.
- Pay close attention to the adjectives the writer uses. Verbs often have connotations, too.

Here is an excerpt from a short story. Several words are circled that help form an image of one character. What image do you get of Mrs. Higgins?

Model

Mrs. Higgins must have been going to bed when he telephoned, for her hair was tucked in loosely under her hat, and her hand at her throat held her light coat tightly across her chest so her dress would not show. She came in, (large) and (plump,) with (a little smile) on her (friendly face). Most of the store lights had been turned out and at first she did not see Alfred, who was standing in the shadow at the end of the counter. Yet as soon as she saw him she did not look as Alfred thought she would look: she smiled, her (blue eyes) never wavered, and with a calmness and dignity that made them forget that her clothes seemed to have been thrown on her, she put out her hand to Mr. Carr and said politely, "I'm Mrs. Higgins. I'm Alfred's mother."

— physical characteristics

—*from* All the Years of Her Life, *Morley Callaghan*

Think about It

What connotations do you understand from the word "plump"? What other words could the author have used? Do you think "plump" was an appropriate choice? Why?

Use the Anthology

Read "Confessions of a Freak" (pages 32-33) and find words that help create an impression of the kind of person the writer is. What connotation do those words have for you?

Activities

1. Choose a favourite song, or a few songs by a favourite artist. Make a list of all the words and phrases that you find which you think are effective. Which of these words have connotations that add meaning?

2. Examine a print ad in a magazine or newspaper, or on a billboard. Which of the words have an emotional meaning? Why would advertisers want to use connotative words?

3. Imagine that you have earned a promotion at work. In the role of employer, write a memo that praises your work and explains why you earned the promotion. Use words that effectively describe you and your work.

How to Read Literature

Before You Start

Stories are powerful. They influence our thinking and help us understand more about others and about ourselves. They can share important lessons that help us on our journey through life.

There are many ways to understand literature. One way is to know the elements of the story (such as characterization, plot, conflict, and setting) and to examine how these work together to create the story.

Another way is to respond personally to the story, and to reflect critically about your response.

Before you follow the steps for reading literature, think about these questions:

- What types of literature do you enjoy reading?
- How can thinking about what you read help you in your relationships with other people?
- What piece of literature have you read most recently? What did you think of it? Why?

Do It Yourself

Examining the Elements of Narrative

- **Step 1** Before you read, think about what you already know about this piece of literature. What do you think the story is going to be about?
- **Step 2** Most of the literature you read is narrative. Narratives always tell a story. There are many kinds of narratives, including short stories, novels, plays, and certain kinds of poems.

These are the elements of narrative:

Characters — the people or other imagined beings who are involved in the conflict of a narrative.
- The major character of the narrative is sometimes called the **protagonist**. In legends or fairy tales, the major character is usually called the **hero**.
- The character who opposes the protagonist is called the **antagonist**. In legends or fairy tales, this character is sometimes called the **villain**.
- Minor characters are those with a smaller role.

Setting — the physical geography or **place** of the narrative, and the **time** period in which it is set. The way the setting is described often creates a mood or atmosphere. A short story will have one main setting; a novel may have many.

Plot — what happens in a narrative: a series of actions or events experienced by the characters. Usually it is **conflict** that drives the plot. The main character finds him/herself in a conflict that s/he must solve. Usually, the character has to change in order for the conflict to be resolved.

The plot of a narrative can be divided into parts:
- The opening scene (beginning) — Here we are introduced to the main characters. The writer describes the setting. Often the writer introduces the conflict to make the reader want to continue reading.
- The rising action — This is the series of events or actions in which the protagonist feels the effects of the conflict. Sometimes there are complications or obstacles that create tension and suspense.
- The climax or crisis — The protagonist makes a decision to change, or takes an action to solve the conflict.
- The falling action (denouement) — The conflict is resolved and usually the protagonist changes in a significant way.

Conflict — the struggle (physical, mental, or spiritual) that the main character experiences. Some main types of conflicts are:

- person vs. person (a mental or physical conflict between the characters, for example, a fist fight or a battle for equal opportunity)
- person vs. self (turmoil within the character, for example, a character struggles between affection for a girl his friends do not like and his desire to be accepted by his peers)
- person vs. nature (a struggle with natural forces, for example, a character fights to escape a forest fire)
- person vs. supernatural (a struggle with supernatural forces, for example, a character battles a ghost)
- person vs. society (a struggle with society and social issues, for example, corruption)

Theme — a statement about human nature or life that comes to you from the story, often after you have read it. Most narratives have a theme, but it is usually not stated directly. The reader decides what the theme is by thinking about a significant truth about human nature or life that the story reveals.

Try not to confuse a topic and a theme. A topic is what the story may be about (for example, friendship). A theme would be "Friends can lead you to ruin if you don't have a strong sense of yourself." That's a truth about human nature that you might learn from reading a story about friends.

Narrative point of view — from which position (through a character's direct telling or not) a story is told. There are two main narrative points of view:

- first-person: a particular character tells the story; the writer uses "I"
- third-person: no particular character tells the story; the writer uses third person (he/she/it) to show the characters' thoughts and actions

Step 3 Read the piece again. Take notes to identify each element of the kind of literature you are reading, based on the information in Step 2.

Step 4 Write an analysis (see also How to Analyze Longer Prose Works, page 16) explaining what the story means, using each of the narrative elements in your explanation.

Do It Yourself

Understanding Literature through Personal Response

- **Step 1** Choose a narrative to read, or read one that your teacher assigns. From the title and any other features, consider what the narrative is about, and how you feel about the subject.

   Read the narrative a first time. In your reading response journal, write a brief paragraph (including questions) that gives your first reaction to the story: what you liked about it, what you didn't like about it, what confused or puzzled you, how you felt about the characters, how you felt about the outcome of the story and how the conflict was solved.

- **Step 2** Read your response to yourself. Underline any questions you have asked.

- **Step 3** Read the narrative a second time. Keep in mind the questions you asked or what puzzled you in your first response. Now write a second paragraph to answer some of the following questions:

   How is the protagonist like or unlike myself?
   How is the protagonist like someone I know?
   How is the conflict like or similar to one I've experienced?
   Who else do I know who has experienced this conflict?
   How did I solve this problem when I encountered it?
   How would I have solved this problem if it had happened to me?
   How did the protagonist change?
   How would I change if this had happened to me?
   What did the events of the story teach the protagonist about life or about human beings?
   What would I identify as the theme of the story?

- **Step 4** Reread both of your response paragraphs. Highlight what you think are the most important points or most insightful comments you've made about the story. Use these points to write one final paragraph about the meaning of the story.

Hot tips

- As you read, try to see the story happening before your eyes, as if it were a movie.

Here are a novel excerpt and a personal response to it. Skim the excerpt to find the main character and the setting.

Model 1

Chapter One/Odette

introduction establishes husband-wife relationship and establishes setting (time, place, and atmosphere)

It's five o'clock in the morning and time for me to go. My husband is turned away from me, sleeping soundly. I move carefully so I don't wake him, pick up my clothes beside the bed, and tiptoe from the room. I suppose if he were to sit up and plead gently, "Don't go, Odette, you don't have to go," I would hesitate and then I would stay. But no, I wouldn't stay.

first-person narration

I dress quickly in the downstairs bathroom, being careful not to make any noise. When I first announced that I was travelling back to see my property in Alberta, willed to me by my mother, Roger was so angry. I didn't dare talk about it. He went into one of his moods, scarcely talking to me, as if I was not worth the effort. He'll get over it, he always does. It's something I've learned to live with, though it was hard at first.

journey theme is introduced;

For the past three days, I've been preparing one-person meals for him, lasagna, chili, hamburger casserole, and steaks and chops, with directions for what to eat with each. When he saw that I was serious about this, he decided he'd take a week off work then and sail his boat up to the Queen Charlottes. I suggested he take one of his fishing buddies along. So he's been looking forward to that, sailing in his precious boat, which he refurbished himself, his pride and joy. I haven't shared his pleasure in sailing because I'm a prairie girl who didn't learn how to swim. He doesn't understand my fear of water; he figures I should enjoy doing what he likes, never thinking that I might prefer other things.

In the kitchen, my domain, hazy with the early morning sunlight, I scribble a note to him, reminding him of things to take along on his fishing trip, telling him the milk delivery has been cancelled, the neighbours will pick up the mail, and all my summer piano students have been informed. I attach the note to the fridge door with a magnet and look at it: no fond word of farewell, just practical matters. Then, silently, I leave, closing and locking the door behind me.

the door symbolizes an end to this part of her life

— from Counterpoint, *by Marie Moser*

Model 2

two main characters — This excerpt immediately created an impression of the two main characters for me. Odette describes her relationship with her husband. She refers to "his precious boat" as though she thinks Roger cares more about it than he does about her. Her description of her husband's moods shows the strain between Roger and Odette. Odette feels worthless and Roger is portrayed as a spoiled child. *— reader's view of main characters*

A friend of mine is in a relationship like this one. I think she, like Odette, needs to be an equal partner, to gain a sense of herself, and to enjoy her — *how protagonist is like someone the reader knows* time alone and her time with him.

how protagonist changes — The protagonist appears to change as she tells her story. I have the impression that by writing her thoughts she discovers something new about herself. As she describes her husband's reaction to her wanting to visit Alberta, I think it becomes clear to Odette how intrusive her relationship has become.

reader's idea of meaning of story — Odette and Roger are dependent on one another for a variety of everyday rituals; however, both struggle to become independent. Roger seeks his "precious boat" for a time alone or with his "fishing buddies." Odette has opened and closed the door as she struggles for her independence.

Think about It

Write a personal response to the model, focusing on the relationship between the husband and wife.

Use the Anthology

Read the excerpt from "Drop the Beat" (pages 210-218). How does the description of each setting affect how you react to each scene?

Activities

1. Choose a narrative from the anthology to analyze. Read it carefully. Then write an analysis of the narrative elements of the story. Use the following questions as a basis for your analysis:

   a. Who are the characters? Describe each. Do a character sketch of the protagonist (see How to Write a Character Sketch, pages 37-41).

   b. What is the conflict? When do you first realize this?

   c. Where and when does the story occur? How would you describe the mood of the story?

   d. Is the story in chronological order? Does it go backward or forward in time? How does the order of the story make you feel?

   e. Is there any dialogue? Does it sound realistic to you? Explain.

   f. What is the narrative point of view?

   g. What is the overall theme of the story? What does this theme mean to you?

2. Choose a play from the anthology. Read it carefully, then write a personal response to it.

How to Write a Character Sketch

Before You Start

In most stories it is the characters that move the action forward. If the characters are strong and believable, the story will be, too. A character sketch is a tool that helps you think about how and why the character acts, and how important points about the character's actions create and resolve the conflict of the story.

Authors reveal important things about a character by:
— describing physical appearance and manner
— what the character says and how he or she says it
— showing the character's strengths and weaknesses through his or her actions
— what other characters say about the character
— the character's inner thoughts about himself or herself and others.

A character sketch is a paragraph or series of paragraphs that describe a character in a story.

Before you follow these steps to write a character sketch, think about these questions:
- What kinds of characters do you like? Dislike?
- What characters have you read about that remind you of yourself? What character traits do you share?

Do It Yourself

> **Step 1** Gather information for a character sketch, using a diagram like the one on the next page. (You can also get a copy of this diagram from your teacher.)

Making It Work: Literature Studies and Reading

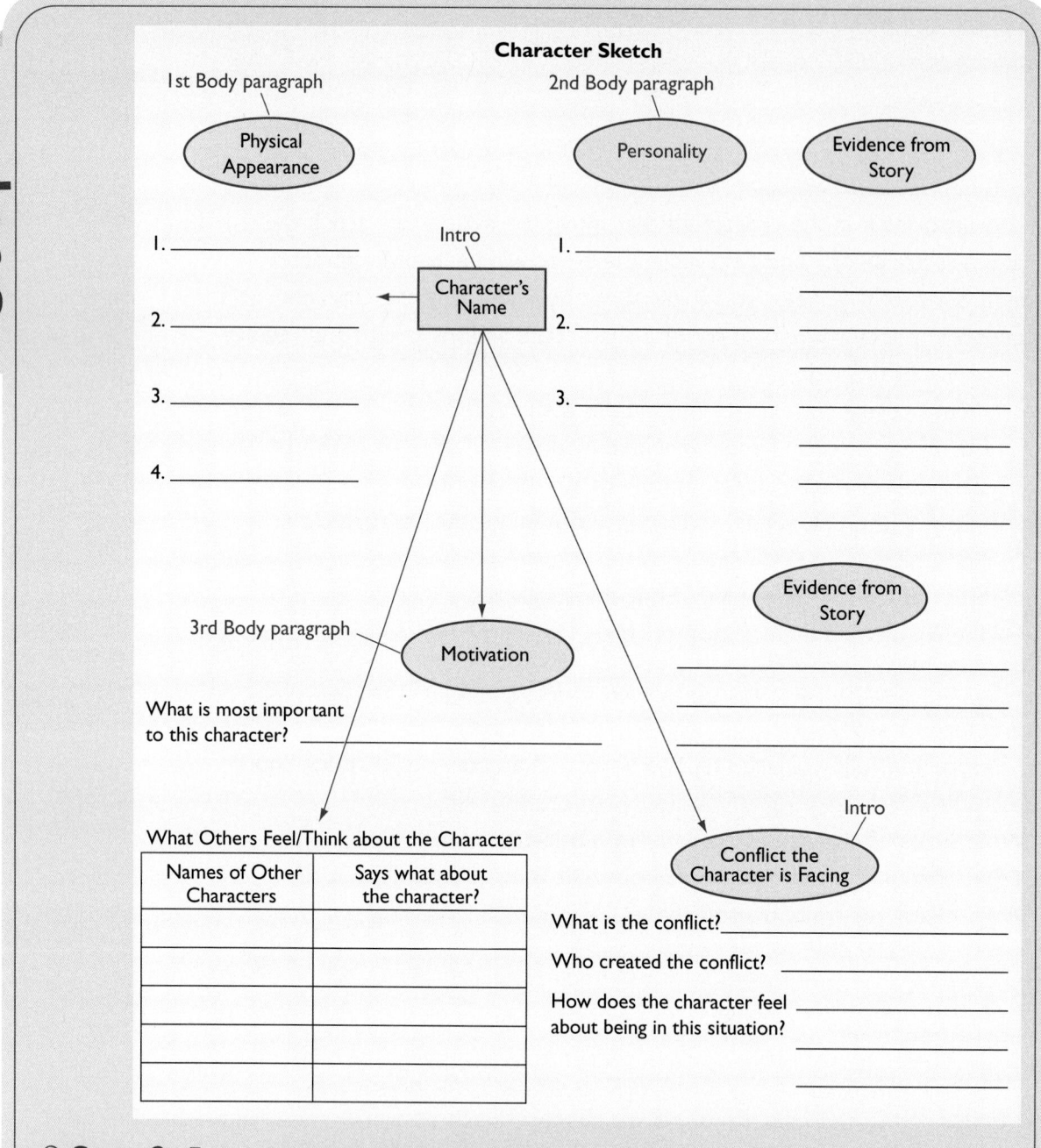

Character Sketch

1st Body paragraph — (Physical Appearance)

2nd Body paragraph — (Personality) — (Evidence from Story)

Intro → Character's Name

1. _____
2. _____
3. _____
4. _____

1. _____
2. _____
3. _____

_____
_____
_____
_____
_____
_____
_____

(Evidence from Story)

3rd Body paragraph — (Motivation)

What is most important to this character? _____

_____
_____
_____
_____

What Others Feel/Think about the Character

Names of Other Characters	Says what about the character?

Intro → Conflict the Character is Facing

What is the conflict? _____
Who created the conflict? _____
How does the character feel _____
about being in this situation?
_____
_____

● **Step 2** Examine your outline. Have you gathered all necessary details about the character? Fill in any missing information.

- **Step 3** Write a draft of your character sketch, using information from your outline. Organize your sketch into paragraphs using the suggestions below.

  Introduction
  Identify the character and the title of the text where the character appears.
  Briefly describe the character's situation and conflict.

  Body Paragraph 1
  Describe the character's physical appearance.

  Body Paragraph 2
  Describe the character's personality, with evidence from the story.

  Body Paragraph 3
  Include other information that you think is important, such as the character's motivation.

  Conclusion
  Explain why the character acts as he or she does in the story, or, if you haven't yet finished the story, predict what the character will do to solve the conflict.

- **Step 4** Revise your draft, checking for spelling, grammar, and correct word usage.

Hot tips

- Brainstorm a variety of adjectives that could be used to describe the character.
- Be aware of the character's actions and manners.
- Decide as you read how the author feels about the character.
- Decide how you feel about the character.
- Look for the character's strengths and weaknesses.

Here is a sample of a character sketch. What do you learn right away about the character?

Model

name of character
title of book
Deanna Wolfe is the main character in Barbara Kingsolver's *Prodigal Summer*. Living alone and working as a forest ranger, she finds the solitary existence she loves threatened by the intrusion of hunters seeking the stealthy coyote families thought to live in her woods.

character's physical characteristics
Deanna is in her 40s, with long, dark, grey-streaked hair. She is tall, slim, and muscular.

character's personality traits
supporting details
additional information
Deanna has a keen understanding of, and love for, nature. She uses nature's signs both on the land (animal tracks and waste) and in the sky (shifting winds, the smell of rain) to measure the pace of her days. She delights in nature's daily changes (new flowers in bloom). She is, however, uncomfortable with other people (she makes sure to be out of her cabin when her monthly food and mail delivery arrives). At the same time, she is attracted both physically and emotionally to Eddie Bondo, the hunter who suddenly appears on her land one day.

character's conflict
Deanna is fascinated by coyotes and their societies, and desperately wants to be sure they can safely survive in the wild. But while she seeks them to observe them, she fears Eddie has come to kill them. She is torn between her love for nature and her love for Eddie; her understanding of coyotes, and his understanding of them.

conclusion
Deanna acts the only way she knows how: she acts to preserve herself and other species, while knowing she must give up something along the way.

Think about It

What is interesting about the character described in the model? Would you like to read the novel to find out more about her? Why?

Use the Anthology

Write a character sketch for the main character in "Bliss at the Burger Bar" (pages 65-72).

Activities

1. Write a character sketch, using the framework on pages 38-39, for:
    a. a television character
    b. a movie character
    c. a character from a short story
    d. a character from a novel

2. Write a synopsis for a short story that you want to sell. Include character sketches of the main characters, as well as notes about the plot and the conflict.

Making It Work: Literature Studies and Reading

How to Read Visual Information

Before You Start

Charts, diagrams, graphs, maps, and photographs give information in a different form and can make it easier to understand and remember. Knowing how to understand the visuals that you see in newspapers, magazines, brochures, annual reports, and so on helps you gain as much information as possible from what you are reading.

Before you follow these steps to reading visuals, think about the questions below:

- What have you read recently that included visual information? What did you learn from it?
- What kinds of items do you read that include visual information? Do you always read the visual information included? Why?
- What kinds of visual information usually catch your eye? Why?
- What kinds of visual information might you see or read in the workplace?

Do It Yourself

Step 1 Before you begin reading visuals, you need to know more about different kinds of visuals.

- A **table** is divided into labelled columns (down) and rows (across). Tables are used for displaying schedules and showing the conversion of one quantity or distance to another. Tables help to show relationships in a more concise way than words can. You usually read these from the top down.
- A visual that is not a table is a **figure**. A figure is usually read from the bottom up.
- A **chart** shows the relationship between categories of information. At work, you may see flow charts which show steps or chains of command, and have labels to make them easy to read. There are many different types of charts.

- A **diagram** shows objects as pictures. A diagram might show how something is made, how it works, or how its parts relate to one another. Maps and illustrations are diagrams.
- A **graph** shows numbers in a visual way.

    A *bar graph* uses bars on a grid to illustrate the sizes or quantities of things. The bars can be horizontal or vertical.

    A *line graph* traces the growth or change in something over a period of time. The time periods are usually indicated on the bottom or top, and the units being measured are along the left side from the bottom to the top. Some line graphs might show changes in different items by giving each one a different colour or kind of line.

    A *circle graph* divides information into sections. It looks like a pie and is also called a pie chart. It shows the relative size of the parts of the whole pie.
- A **photograph** is a creative, artistic way to add images and sometimes colour to a report. A photograph often has a caption (or cutline) underneath explaining or describing the photograph. A photo essay might include a deck. A deck is a section of text, printed in large type, that introduces a photo essay or an article.

- **Step 2** Choose a text that includes visual information, or read one that your teacher assigns. Identify the type of visual, using the information from Step 1.
- **Step 3** Read the title (if there is one) of the visual to learn what it is about.
- **Step 4** Be sure to read any captions or additional information that is included with the visual.
- **Step 5** Read the visual by carefully considering its purpose. Ask: What is the writer explaining with this visual? What important details does it provide to help me understand the text? What does it help me to see?

HOT tips

- In books, the visuals are often numbered by chapter, so Figure 5.2 is the second figure in chapter 5.

As you read the following visuals, think about why the format is best suited for the information.

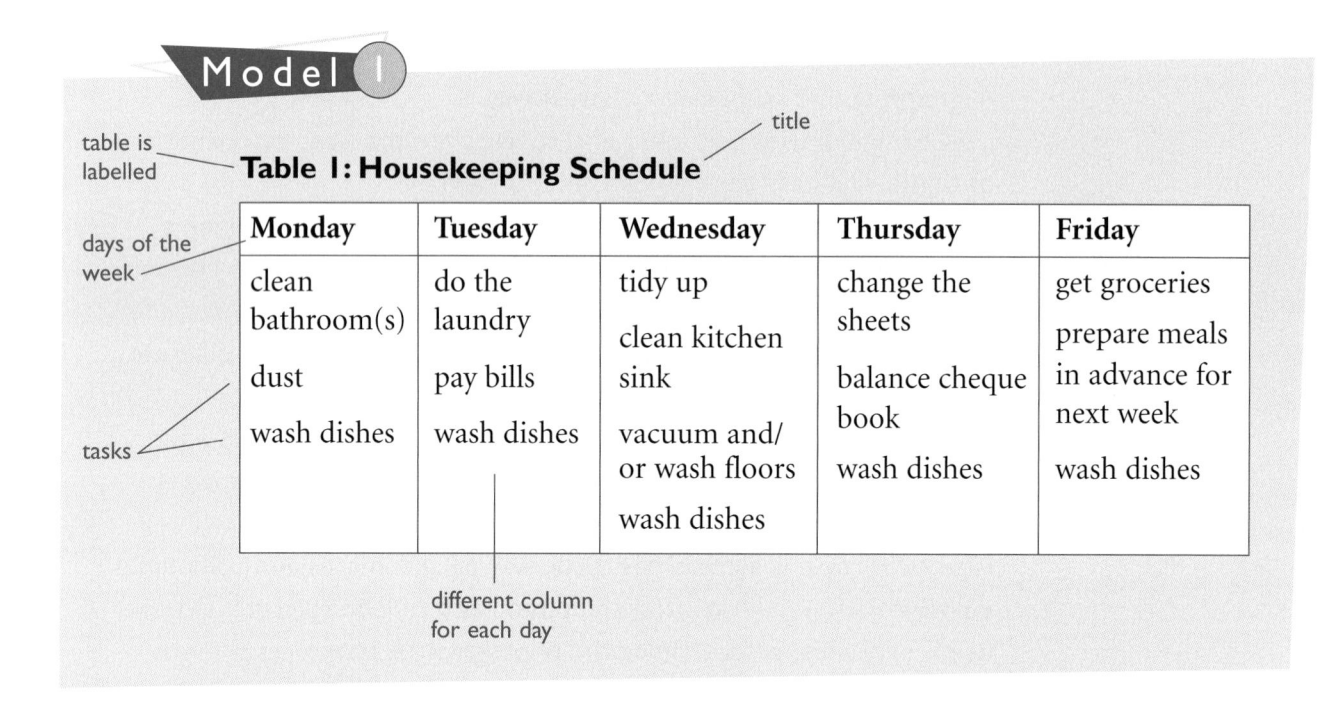

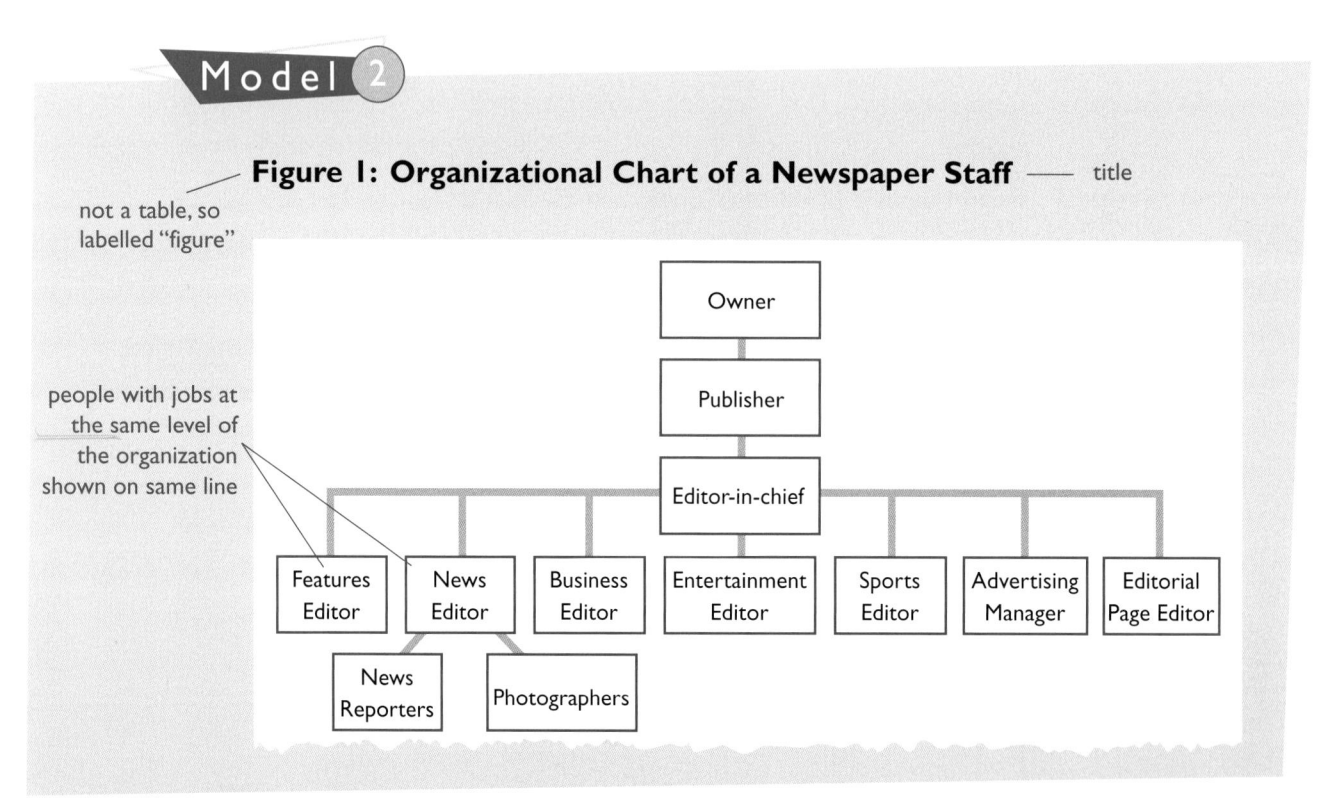

Model 1

Table 1: Housekeeping Schedule — title

table is labelled

days of the week

Monday	Tuesday	Wednesday	Thursday	Friday
clean bathroom(s)	do the laundry	tidy up	change the sheets	get groceries
dust	pay bills	clean kitchen sink	balance cheque book	prepare meals in advance for next week
wash dishes	wash dishes	vacuum and/or wash floors	wash dishes	wash dishes
		wash dishes		

tasks

different column for each day

Model 2

Figure 1: Organizational Chart of a Newspaper Staff — title

not a table, so labelled "figure"

people with jobs at the same level of the organization shown on same line

- Owner
  - Publisher
    - Editor-in-chief
      - Features Editor
      - News Editor
        - News Reporters
        - Photographers
      - Business Editor
      - Entertainment Editor
      - Sports Editor
      - Advertising Manager
      - Editorial Page Editor

How to Read Visual Information

Model 3

Figure 2: Weather Map

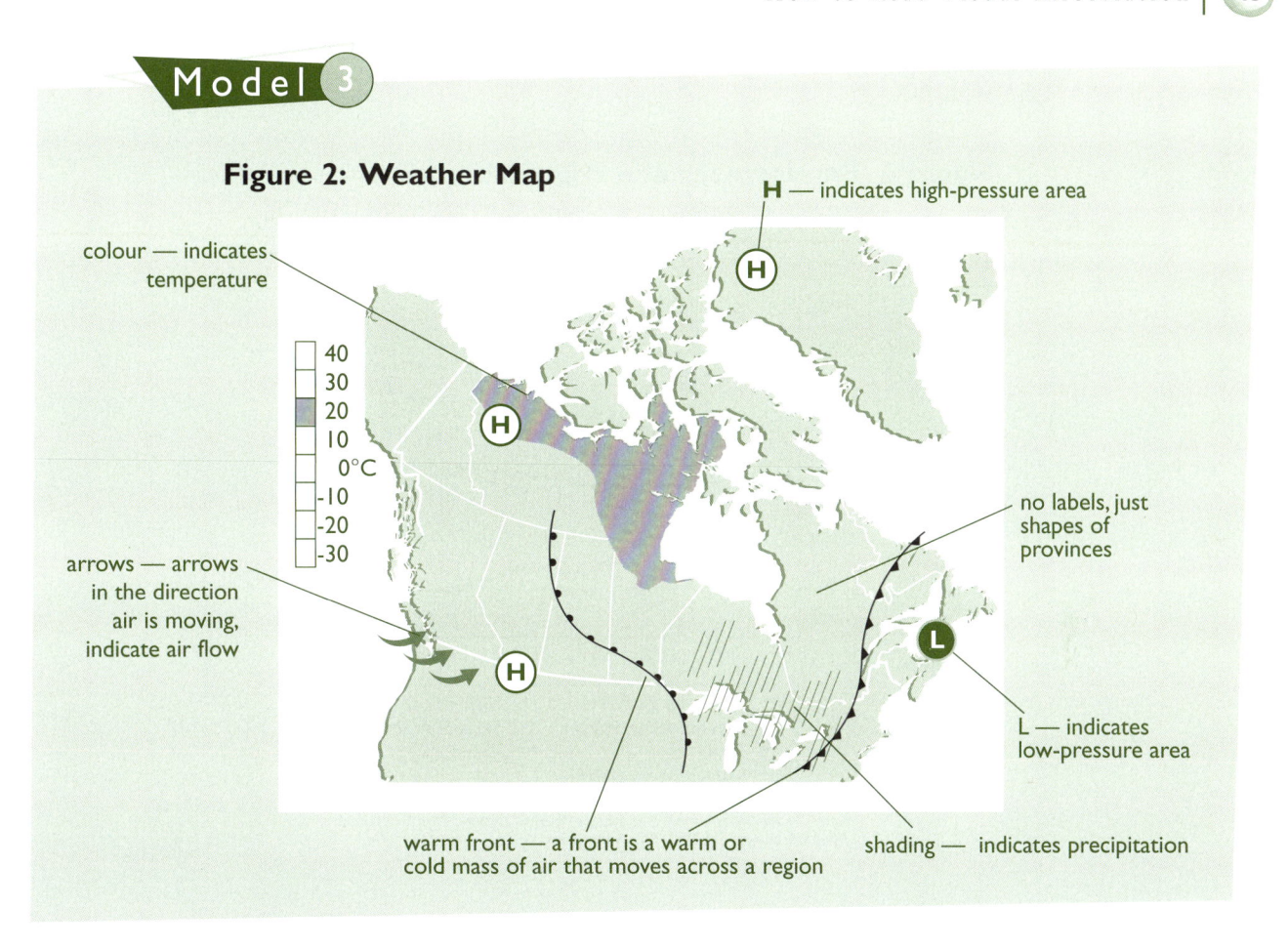

- **H** — indicates high-pressure area
- colour — indicates temperature
- arrows — arrows in the direction air is moving, indicate air flow
- no labels, just shapes of provinces
- **L** — indicates low-pressure area
- warm front — a front is a warm or cold mass of air that moves across a region
- shading — indicates precipitation

Model 4

Figure 3: Television-Viewing Habits — title

- number of hours
- Number of hours per day
- results
- names of those surveyed: Alex, Arnel, Ambrose, Bob, Catherine, Darcy, Guy, Marci, Nulla, Randy

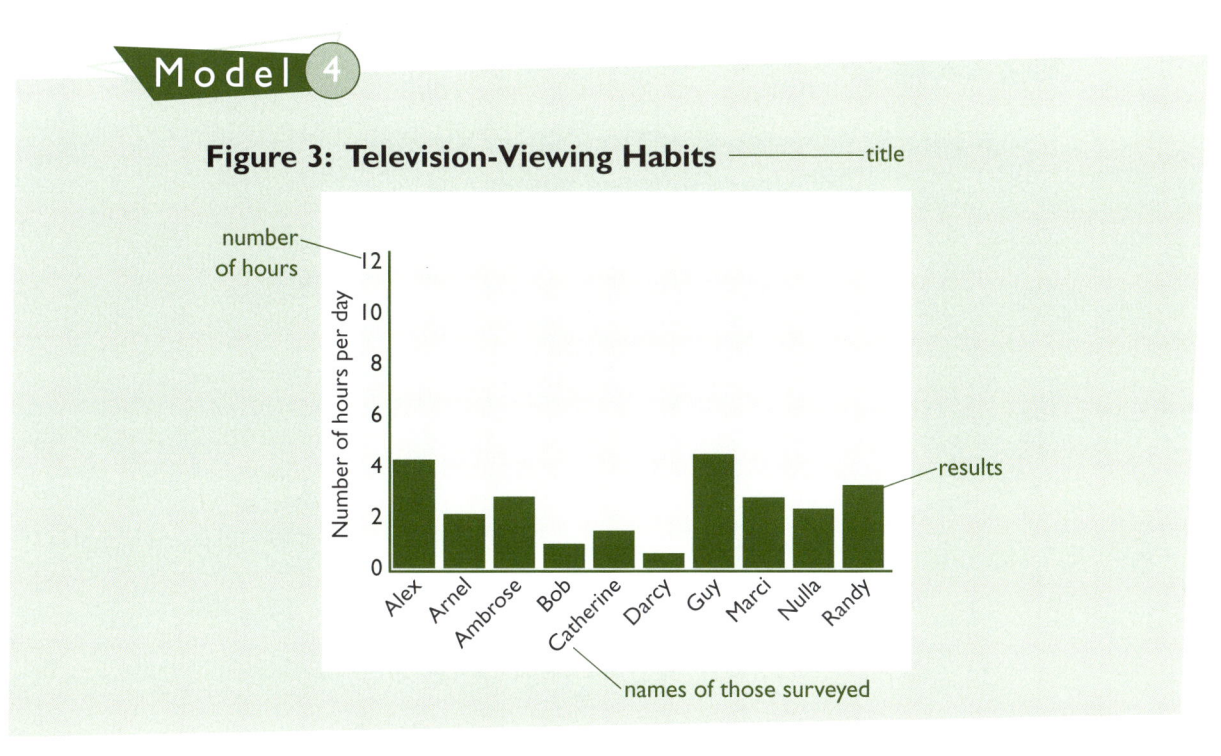

Making It Work: Literature Studies and Reading

Model 5

Figure 4: Employment and Education ———— title
(growth or decline in employment, by education level)

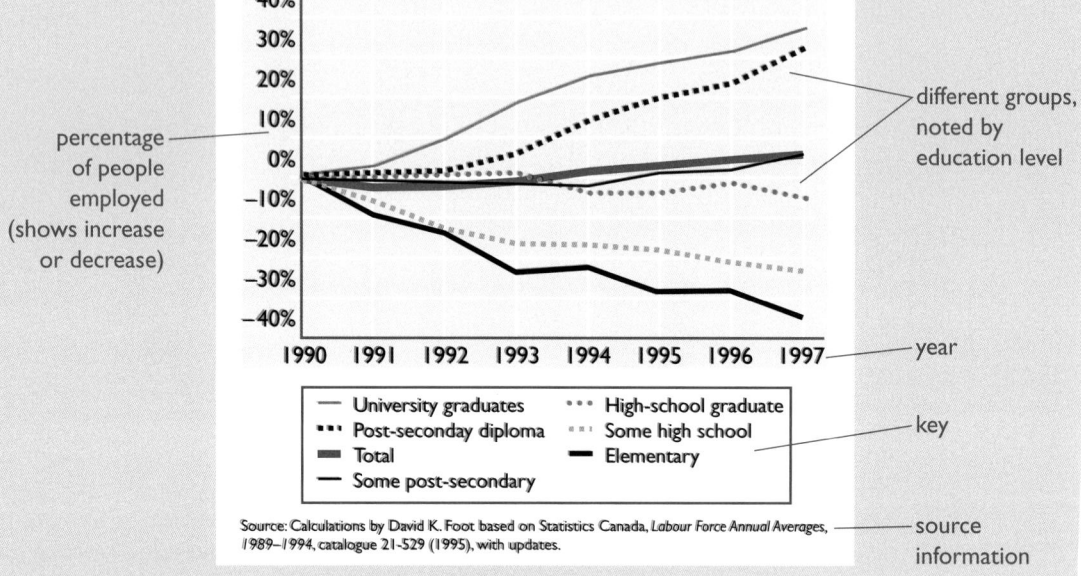

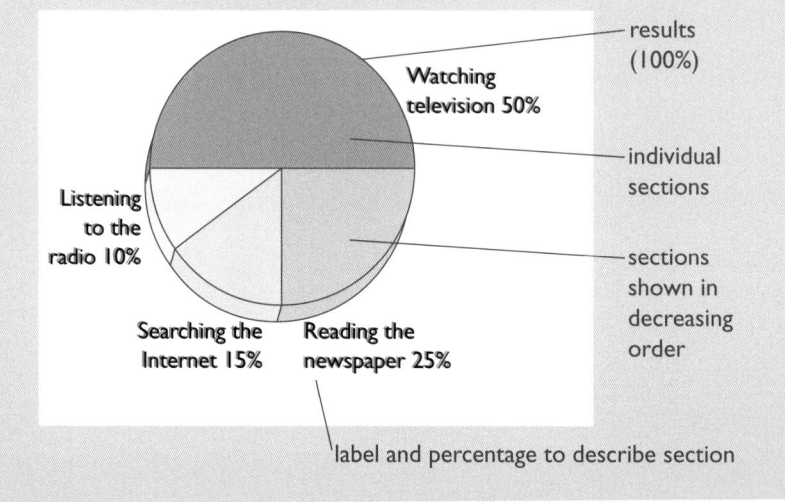

percentage of people employed (shows increase or decrease)

different groups, noted by education level

year

— University graduates   ··· High-school graduate
··· Post-seconday diploma   ··· Some high school   key
— Total   — Elementary
— Some post-secondary

Source: Calculations by David K. Foot based on Statistics Canada, *Labour Force Annual Averages*, 1989–1994, catalogue 21-529 (1995), with updates. ———— source information

Model 6

Figure 5: Percentage of Time Spent Viewing Different Forms of Media ———— title

results (100%)

Watching television 50%

individual sections

Listening to the radio 10%

sections shown in decreasing order

Searching the Internet 15%   Reading the newspaper 25%

label and percentage to describe section

Think about It

What kind of information do you expect to get from each of the models shown on pages 44-47 (comparisons, change over time, process, and so on)?

Use the Anthology

Look at the chart "Taking Everything into Account" (pages 154-155). Why do you think this information was presented in a chart? Do you think there is a more effective way to present it? Explain.

Activities

1. Survey your friends about their media-viewing and -listening habits and graph your results. Then survey and graph the habits of an older audience. Consider distinguishing between men and women. Explain the significance of your findings.

2. Find examples of other kinds of visuals. What elements do they include (for example, titles, captions, labels, and so on)? Do the elements of the visuals you found help you to understand the information more easily? Why?

Writing

TABLE OF CONTENTS

The Writing Process	50
How to Research	54
How to Write a Paragraph	58
How to Write an Opinion Paper	62
How to Write a Report	67
How to Write a Formal Letter	70
How to Write a Résumé	76
How to Write a Covering Letter	83
How to Write and Send E-mail	89

The Writing Process

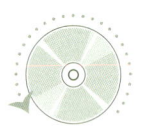

Writing, like any kind of creation, doesn't just happen. Writing is a process that takes time and thought. Almost every time you write something, you go through some — or all — of the steps in the writing process.

The Writing Process

Choose a format and topic
⬇
Generate ideas
⬇
Write a first draft
⬇
Revise on your own
⬇
Revise with a partner, where possible
⬇
Write the final version

▶ Choose a format and topic

Decide on your topic — either something that interests you or something that has been assigned to you.

Choose the writing format you will use: opinion paper, response paper, descriptive paragraph, narrative, explanation, report, formal essay, or familiar essay.

Decide who your audience will be. Understanding who will be reading your work will help you decide how formal it should be and what type of language you should use.

▶ Generate ideas

Begin by brainstorming all the ideas you might want to develop in your writing piece. Share your ideas with someone else to make sure that you have included everything you need.

Begin to put your ideas in order so that you save the strongest point, most interesting idea, most exciting anecdote, or most convincing argument for the end.

▶ Write a first draft

Using the order you designed as a guideline, begin to write your piece. A computer is useful because it allows you to change words, move sentences and paragraphs, and remove or rewrite text easily and effortlessly.

In your first draft, don't worry about spelling, grammar, punctuation, or typing errors. Just keep writing until you feel you are finished.

▸ Revise on your own

This part of the process involves four steps.

First, revise for content. Ask:

- Does the writing say what I wanted it to say?
- Have I repeated ideas unnecessarily?
- Are the ideas in a logical, easy-to-follow order?

Delete any ideas that repeat, ramble, and don't connect with the rest of the writing. Make your introduction and conclusion as strong as you can. Ensure that facts and figures are correct and that sources are properly cited.

Next, revise for vocabulary.

Circle words that you have repeated many times and use a thesaurus to replace them with synonyms. Find any words that are too simple (for example, said) and replace them with words that are more sophisticated (for example, shouted, cried, or yelled). Read over your work to make sure that you have not over-edited. The writing should still sound like you.

Next, revise for structure.

- Does your writing piece follow the conventions of the format (for example, an essay has an introduction, a body, and a conclusion)?
- Do your paragraphs have all of the elements they need?
- Have you separated different topics into different paragraphs?
- Have you used a variety of sentence structures (simple, complex, compound)?

Finally, revise for spelling and grammar.

If you're using a computer, use a spell-check or grammar-check feature, remembering that these features won't catch all mistakes. Make sure to check punctuation and capitalization. Check the spelling of any words that usually give you trouble. Check for misspelled versions of their/there/they're and to/too/two.

▸ Revise with a partner

Choose someone with whom you are comfortable and from whom you can accept criticism.

Have your partner read the piece silently and give a quick opinion without thinking too much. Then have your partner read the piece out loud to make sure the words flow smoothly.

Ask your partner to comment on the following:

- Format — Does it follow the appropriate structure?
- Tone — What is the tone of the piece? Is that the tone you had in mind?
- Vocabulary — Is it appropriate? Is it too formal or informal?
- Sentence structure — Do the sentences flow well? Is the writing too choppy or does it ramble too much?

▸ Write the final version

Once you have completed all the steps of editing; type, rewrite, or print out your final version. Choose a font that is clear, distinct, and easy to read.

How to Research

Before You Start

Research involves looking for information from a variety of sources. You might do research for school (for example, for an essay on a career in sports), for personal reasons (for example, to find a used car), or in the workplace (for example, to find out how customers use your company's product). Although sources change, the skills stay the same.

Before you follow the steps to research, think about these questions:
- What research sources have you found helpful recently?
- What challenges did you face with your most recent research?

Do It Yourself

Steps

- **Step 1** Determine the topic of your research. If you have a choice, choose a topic that interests you, or one that you would like to know more about.

- **Step 2** In a simple sentence clearly state the purpose for your research:

    I want to find information about a career in drywalling.
    I want to find information about buying a used car.
    I want to find information about travelling to Barbados.
    I want to find information on the topic of the Young Offenders laws.

- **Step 3** Identify the sources you'll go to for information — newspapers, magazines, the Internet, people, books, and so on. You might find that the information that's available forces you to change or adjust your topic. For example, you may find more current information about a topic related to the one you chose rather than about the one you chose. Make any changes in topic you think are necessary.
    - If you are researching a career, consider getting information from the Guidance Department at your school, an employment or job skills training centre, a union office, someone who works in this career, the Internet, or job ads.

- If you are researching a purchase, know your price range, and consider getting information from a store that sells the item, books, articles, the Internet, newspaper ads, and so on.
- If you are researching travel, know your bugdet and travel dates, and consider getting information from a travel agent, books, articles, pamphlets, newspaper ads, the Internet, or someone who has travelled to this location.
- If you are researching a topic for a report, consider getting information from books, articles, outside agencies, special interest groups, experts, or the Internet. Consider where you might be able to get support material, such as visuals and samples.

Step 4 Keep clear, accurate, and detailed notes. Record your information on 3 × 5 cards. Your notes should include information about the source so that you can cite it (refer to it) in your work. Get as much information about your source as you can. This way, you or someone else can return to it or check it to be sure that you were accurate.

To cite a book, you will need the author's name, the book title, the name of the publisher, and the date and city of publication. To cite a magazine or newspaper, you will need the title of the article, the author's name, the title of the publication, and the date or issue number of the publication. To cite a Web site, you will need the name of the site, the URL of the site, the name of the author of any information that you have used, and perhaps the date that you found the information. To cite video or film, you will need the title, the name of the producer and the distributor, and possibly the date of production.

You may cite your references within your report, where you have used their information. You can also provide a complete list of sources at the end of your report. Use a style guide that your teacher recommends.

Step 5 Once you have gathered all your information, spread out your cards in front of you. Move them around until the information is organized in a way that presents all the facts clearly.

Step 6 Follow the steps of the writing process (see pages 50-53) to write a report, summary, article, or opinion paper to share the information you have found.

Making It Work: Writing

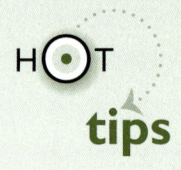

Hot tips

- Brainstorm a variety of research topics and then narrow your focus.
- Remember to verify information found on the Internet — anybody can post anything on the Web, and information may not be correct. (For more about Internet research, see How to Search on the Internet, page 150-153.)
- Cite all sources for any information you find and use — whether it's from a book, a magazine, or the Internet.

Here are some sources that you might use to research. As you read them, think about what kind of information you might be trying to get from each one. Why is that source a good one for the information you seek?

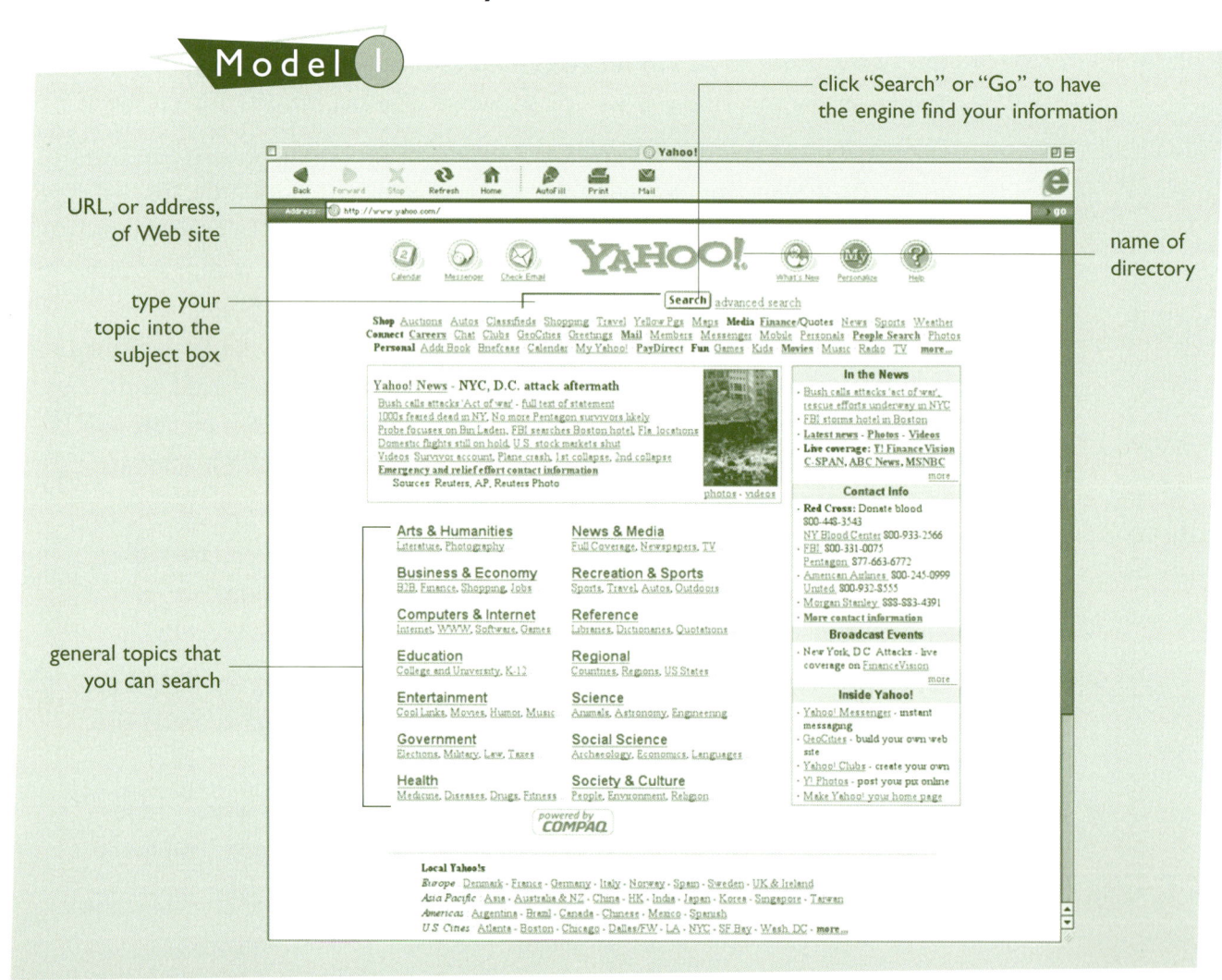

Model 1

Screenshot of the Yahoo! homepage with the following annotations:

- URL, or address, of Web site
- type your topic into the subject box
- general topics that you can search
- click "Search" or "Go" to have the engine find your information
- name of directory

Model 2

The Daily — title and date of newspaper
CLASSIFIED   February 22, 2002

AUTOMOTIVE — title of classified section

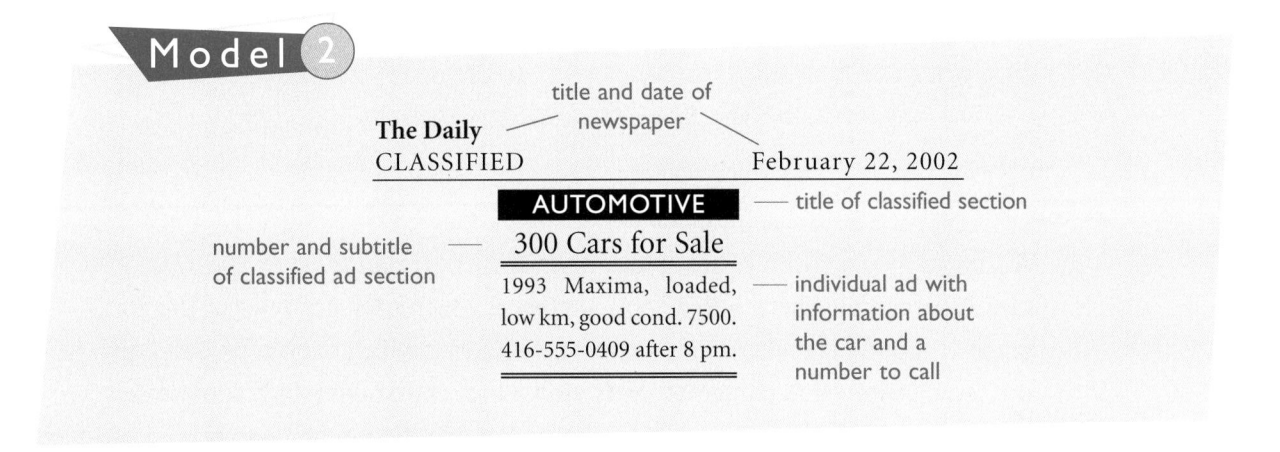

number and subtitle of classified ad section — 300 Cars for Sale

1993 Maxima, loaded, low km, good cond. 7500. 416-555-0409 after 8 pm. — individual ad with information about the car and a number to call

Think about It

If you wanted to learn more about the car advertised in the newspaper model above, what key words might you use in an Internet search?

Use the Anthology

The anthology includes classified ads (pages 84-88); Web pages (pages 208-209); and travel brochures (pages 222-227 and pages 235-238). You can use all of these sources for research. What characteristics of the format of each source make the source useful for research? Are some sources of information easier to use than others? Why?

Activity

1. Choose a topic of interest to you that is related to the world of work. Begin an Internet search for information about this topic (see How to Search on the Internet, pages 150-153). Keep accurate information about where you find the details. Search for at least five pieces of information. Discuss why you think the source is reliable or why it might be a source you need to question.

How to Write a Paragraph

Before You Start

A paragraph is a group of sentences that focuses on one topic or one main idea. A paragraph starts with a topic sentence, which tells clearly what the paragraph is about. Next come one or more sentences which explain or develop the topic sentence. A paragraph ends with a final statement which summarizes, restates, or links the paragraph to a similar topic in the next paragraph.

Before you follow the steps to write a paragraph, think about these questions:
- What do you already know about paragraphs?
- What kind of paragraphs can you see yourself having to write in the workplace?

Do It Yourself

Step 1 Choose a topic for your paragraph. Think about how you feel about the topic and how you are going to share your ideas. Then think about the audience for whom you are writing. Write your topic sentence.

Step 2 Brainstorm and list all of the ideas you want to include in your paragraph.

Step 3 Decide on the order of your ideas. Which idea describes your topic? Which idea should come next? Which idea should come after that? Use linking words to connect the ideas in your paragraph. The last sentence before your final sentence should be the idea that best and most clearly supports your topic sentence.

If you are writing more than one paragraph, you can include one main idea for each paragraph. Begin with a paragraph that introduces your topic. Next, decide on the order of the paragraphs so that they support your topic. Finish with a paragraph that summarizes your topic. For each paragraph, follow the steps listed here.

- **Step 4** Write your concluding statement if necessary (see expository paragraph, below). Make sure it summarizes and restates your topic sentence and that it doesn't include any new information or new ideas.
- **Step 5** Re-read and revise your work. Check to make sure that you have used complete sentences, that the order you have used makes sense, and that the purpose and supporting details of your paragraph are clear. If you like, have someone else read it as well. Check for, and correct, any grammar and spelling errors.
- **Step 6** Write your final version.

HOT tips

- There are three main types of paragraphs:

    A **narrative** paragraph tells a story and pays particular attention to character, setting, and conflict.

    A **descriptive** paragraph gives a single impression of something to the reader. It uses many details to create a vivid picture and appeals to the senses.

    An **expository** paragraph explains. It gives information and should be clear, factual, and straightforward. It includes a concluding sentence.

- For an expository paragraph, consider giving information by comparing and contrasting (telling how things are similar and different), by using cause and effect (using facts and examples to support what you write), or by giving an opinion.

Making It Work: Writing

Here is a model of each of the three kinds of paragraphs. As you read each model, think about the kind of information it gives you.

Model 1

Narrative Paragraph

topic sentence — <u>The plan was about to be realized</u>. Despite great difficulty acquiring parental approval, Sal, Josh, and Gerpet <u>finalized their plans to begin the canoeing adventure</u> they had been planning since they had first met and become close friends in Grade 9. Here they were — high-school graduates at last, 18 years old, and <u>ready to move on to the next phase of their lives, but not without completing the plan.</u>

supporting details

final statement

Model 2

Descriptive Paragraph

many details create a vivid picture

I, who cannot see, find hundreds of things to interest me through mere touch. I feel the <u>delicate symmetry of a leaf</u>. I pass my hands lovingly about the <u>smooth skin of a silver birch</u>, or the <u>rough, shaggy bark of a pine tree</u>. In spring, I touch the branches of trees hopefully in search of a bud, ….

— *from* Three Days to See, *Helen Keller*

Model 3

Expository Paragraph

cause — <u>Poor preparation for classes</u> remains an important reason
effect — <u>why students fail.</u> Preparation for class includes sufficient sleep, good eating habits, and a routine that assures that students will attend classes every day and arrive on time. Unfortunately, <u>students are sidetracked by many other distractions</u> that take — fact
place in their daily lives.

Think about It

In which type of paragraph is it important to use colourful adjectives? Why?

Use the Anthology

You will find paragraphs in many of the selections in the anthology. There are paragraphs in newspaper articles, such as "Rising Threats of Violence in Schools Concern Police" (pages 115-116), short stories such as "Walking" (pages 164-175), and non-fiction pieces, such as "Boom, Bust, & Echo 2000" (pages 37-41). Choose a paragraph from one of the selections in the anthology. What information does it give you? What kind of paragraph is it?

Activities

1. Choose a writing sample that you have previously completed. Select one paragraph that you feel could use some improvement. Follow the steps on pages 58-59 to improve that paragraph.
2. Imagine you have just completed your first day of work at a new job. Follow the steps here to write a paragraph describing your day.
3. Follow the steps to write a paragraph on a topic of your choice.

How to Write an Opinion Paper

Before You Start

An opinion is an idea or a point of view that someone has about a certain topic. One way to share your ideas is in an opinion paper — a piece of writing that communicates and supports your opinion in an organized way. An opinion paper is strongest when it is factual, logical, clear, and unemotional. Most often, people write opinion papers to respond to something they have read or heard, or to share an idea of their own.

Before you follow the steps to write an opinion paper, think about these questions:
- What topics do you have strong opinions about?
- Why would you like to be able to write a strong opinion paper?
- Why might it be important to share your ideas in the workplace? Why would it be important to share them clearly?

Do It Yourself

Steps

- **Step 1** If you are responding to something you have read, read the article or piece of writing several times. Read it carefully. Highlight (with self-stick notes in a book or with a highlighter on a photocopy or clipping) the sections that you think show the topic of the writing, the author's attitude toward the topic, and the key points the author uses to support his or her views.

- **Step 2** Write a topic sentence that clearly outlines the topic for discussion and how you feel about it.

- **Step 3** If you are responding to a piece of writing, plan your response. Do you agree with the author's view? If you do, summarize the points with which you agree, and explain why. Do you disagree with the author's view? If you do, summarize the points with which you disagree, and explain why.

   If you are writing a paper on a topic of your choice, brainstorm and note ideas that support your opinion.

How to Write an Opinion Paper

- **Step 4** Organize your ideas into paragraphs, following the steps in How to Write a Paragraph (pages 58-59). Step 3 explains how to write a group of paragraphs. Use your strongest point as the topic of your last paragraph before the conclusion.
- **Step 5** Write each paragraph, making sure to support your statements with facts, statistics, personal experiences, anecdotes (stories of things that have happened), or with portions that you have highlighted from the piece of writing. Remember to use connecting words between paragraphs to help link your ideas. Make sure that each paragraph helps to support your opinion clearly.
- **Step 6** Write a concluding paragraph. Summarize your opinion, but don't add any new ideas.
- **Step 7** Follow the steps of the writing process (pages 50-53) to revise, edit, and prepare the final version of your opinion paper.

HOT tips

- You may agree with some parts of an article and disagree with others. Be sure to state that in your introduction and restate it in your conclusion.

As you read these models, think about the words that tell you whether the opinion paper is a response to a piece of writing or an expression of someone's point of view on a topic of his or her choice.

Model 1

On Wednesday, April 5th, an article appeared in the *Era-Banner* newspaper entitled "Teen vandals show attitude of the 90's," written by George Snow. As a teenager who lives in the community Mr. Snow wrote about, <u>I take great exception to his generalization that all teenagers are idle vandals</u> who roam the streets looking for an opportunity to vandalize public property.

— writer's opinion

information from the original article — Mr. Snow inaccurately reports that large groups of teenagers regularly vandalize the James Ball Park area by tagging the walls and pulling down the fence around the property. As a regular user of the ball diamond, I have seen one incident of tagging that occurred this past summer. *new facts to support writer's opinion* — The taggers were not teenagers, but two nine-year-old boys who were reported to the police by the coach of my ball team. I checked with the Parks and Recreation Department and learned that there have been no other tagging incidents.

Mr. Snow should check his facts regarding the damage to the fence. This damage was not caused by teen vandals but by the trucking firm whose property is attached to the park. The trucks often back up when loading and back into the fence, as there is little room to turn. I have witnessed this several times while I have been in the park.

While I realize that there are teens who are disrespectful, Mr. Snow needs to understand that many of us appreciate the park and use it appropriately. His facts are incorrect and his reporting is harmful to teen reputations. He has taken incidents out of context and has generalized attitudes that do not exist in all cases. Mr. Snow needs *restatement of writer's opinion* — to have an attitude check and leave teens alone. His article is inaccurate and unfair to the teens of this community.

Model 2

Modelling Ads Mislead Youth

By Morning Star Trickey

Advertising reaches a huge audience — according to marketing statistics research, the average person is bombarded by approximately 7000 broadcast messages daily.

The impact fashion and cosmetic advertising have on youth concerns many people: It sets a standard for attractiveness that most teens, whether consciously or subconsciously, attempt to adhere to. — *writer's opinion*

Critics complain the standards in fashion and cosmetic advertising are unrealistically high. For example, the model in an advertisement is always beautiful, with flawless features and a perfect body. It is unreasonable for anyone to expect to reproduce this contrived appearance.

For instance, Deborah Samuel, one of Canada's top fashion and advertising photographers, says, "A model can spend hours with her hair and makeup alone. It could take several hours to get the right shot. No one should expect to look like that."

comments from different sources to support writer's opinion

In Ms. Samuel's opinion, physical perfection is not something to strive for.

Fashion and cosmetic advertising may also be a contributing factor to a youth's low self-image. Sunshine Martinez, 18, a student at George Harvey C.I., says, "Every girl I know thinks she's fat. Girls have this picture that you have to be a bone rack to be attractive. And I think most fashion advertising reinforces this negative concept."

According to Dr. Elaine Borins, a psychiatrist and the director of The Women's Clinic at Toronto Western Hospital, many advertisements convey this destructive image.

Furthermore, Dr. Borins believes that a certain product can't give a person a certain lifestyle, nor can it give the person happiness. Advertising only shows people what they want to see, and what they would like to be, she says.

If teens think positively of themselves, they will not take seriously the perfect images created by advertising. "Teens follow trends because they are not comfortable with themselves. If you like yourself, then you don't need to look or act like anyone else," says Ms. Samuel.

Danielle Gagnier, a young Toronto model, says that she has considered giving it up. "I felt like a product, not a person. I really think people's expectations are too high. The money is great, but I sometimes feel like I'm being used."

summary of writer's opinion

She also says fashion and cosmetic advertising do seriously affect many teens. Many girls feel inadequate because they don't look like the model in the advertisement. And Ms. Gagnier feels, "Teens really don't need that kind of pressure on them."

Think about It

How are the points of view and tone different in the two sample opinion papers?

Use the Anthology

The article "Why Idalécio's as Canadian as maple syrup" (pages 30-31) is one man's opinion about what makes him Canadian. He is responding to a television ad called I Am Canadian. What words in his opinion piece show you that he is responding to something he has seen or heard?

Activities

1. Read your local newspaper. Choose an editorial or an article that addresses an issue about which you have an opinion. Write an opinion paper which clearly indicates how you feel about the article.

2. Brainstorm a list of issues that are important to you. Choose one and write an opinion paper explaining and supporting your stand on the issue.

How to Write a Report

Before You Start

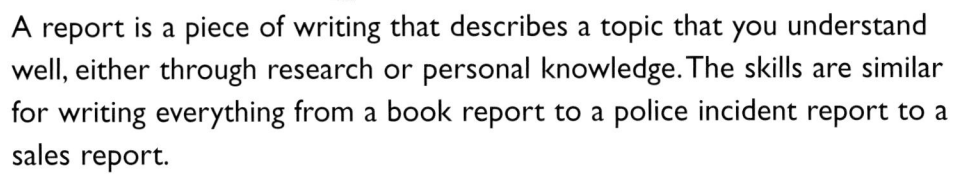

A report is a piece of writing that describes a topic that you understand well, either through research or personal knowledge. The skills are similar for writing everything from a book report to a police incident report to a sales report.

Before you follow the steps to write a report, think about these questions:
- What reports have you read? What did you notice about how they were organized?
- Think of a report you have written recently. What was the topic? What steps did you follow to write it?
- What kind of language do you usually use when you write a report?

Do It Yourself

- **Step 1** State the topic of your report clearly. For example, "In order to become an apprentice in the drywalling trade, there are five important steps you need to follow."

- **Step 2** Gather your information. For some reports, you will need to do research (see How to Research, pages 54-57). For other reports, you will be sharing knowledge that you already have. In either case, take notes about the information you are gathering. List the sources you use (see How to Research, Step 4, page 55)

- **Step 3** Organize your information by placing your notes (recorded on index cards, separate sheets of paper, the computer, and so on) in the order that makes the most sense to you. Just like with a paragraph (see pages 58-59), you want to state your topic, write several paragraphs that describe and explain your topic, and then share your findings.

- **Step 4** Read your information again. Are the steps in the right order? Does the information make sense? Have you given information to prove or back up the statements you made?

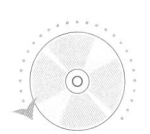

- **Step 5** Conclude your report by restating some of your key points.
- **Step 6** Write a final sentence that gives a conclusion or shares your findings.
- **Step 7** Follow the steps of the writing process (pages 50-53) to revise and edit your report before completing your final version. Make sure to include in your final report a list of sources you have used (see How to Research, Step 4, page 55).

HOT tips

- If your report is long, use subheadings to help the reader.

Here is an example of a report. What do you think makes it different from other kinds of writing?

Model

Droughts and Floods

topic — In many parts of the world, droughts and floods are rare, while some areas of the world are continually plagued by the destruction that droughts and floods can cause.

Millions of people live in dry grassland and partial desert areas where there is little rain, even in a good year. If there is no rain, an entire year's food supply may be lost. If there is no rain for several years, millions of people face starvation. This is what happened across the dry region of Africa in the mid 1970s and 1980s.

— description of topic

While some parts of the world suffer from extreme dryness, other parts of the world face the continual threat of extreme rain. Tropical regions receive much more rain than temperate regions. In these regions, the air is very hot, and it holds a huge amount of water. The combination produces frequent thunderstorms and heavy rains. Most violent are the monsoon rains that sweep into India and Southeast Asia in May and June each year. The rivers cannot cope, resulting in flooding that destroys food supplies and housing and causes the drowning of many animals as well as humans.

Extreme weather conditions, whether they involve no rain or an overabundance of rain, can cause great hardship for those who live in these regions.

— restatement of key points

Think about It

What visual elements could you add to this report to give more information?

Use the Anthology

Read an incident report (pages 176-177). How does that report compare to the report here?

Activities

1. Write a report about a career that interests you. The report must list your information sources and include the following details:
   - a description of the job — exactly what the worker is required to do
   - educational requirements — any requirements, including post-secondary courses or experience (college, apprenticeship)
   - average salary
   - how to apply for the job
   - comments from people who are presently employed in this career

2. Write a short report about one of your co-op placements, or imagine that you have had a job. Describe the job and your responsibilities; the goals you set for yourself; how you tried to achieve those goals; and whether you feel that you did achieve them.

How to Write a Formal Letter

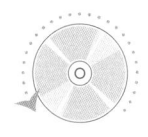

Before You Start

A formal letter is a letter that uses formal language and format. You might write one to go with a résumé, to register a complaint, or to ask for information. A formal letter includes a date, the addresses of the sender and the recipient, a formal greeting (Dear Mrs. Fong, Dear Sir), and a formal closing (Sincerely, Yours truly).

Before you follow the steps to write a formal letter, think about the following:
- What formal letters have you written or received in the past?
- Think of a formal letter that you wrote. What was your purpose in writing it?
- How were the words you used in your formal letter different from words you would use in a note to a friend?

Do It Yourself

Step 1 Write an outline of your letter. Using one line for each, write your name, street address, city and province, and postal code several lines down from the top left corner of the page. Leave two line spaces. Write the date, including the year. Leave two line spaces. Using one line for each, write the recipient's name, company name if any, street address, city and province, and postal code. Leave two line spaces. Write a formal greeting (Dear … ,).

At the top of the page, state the purpose of your letter. Then, think about the reader: Who are you writing to? What position does he or she hold? In the outline, make a note of that person's name, address, and position.

Next, think about the impression you want to give the reader. What is the tone of the letter? What impression of yourself do you want to present? What type of words should you use? The words you choose will set the tone of the letter.

How to Write a Formal Letter

- **Step 2** Brainstorm a list of facts you want to include in the letter. Use the middle of your outline page for this.
- **Step 3** Choose the facts you want to use. You might do this by highlighting or circling the most important points.
- **Step 4** Put your facts in order. What is the most important fact? What is the next important fact?
- **Step 5** Begin writing your letter. In your first sentence, clearly state the purpose of your letter (see Step 1). Sometimes, it's a good idea to make this sentence stand alone to make the greatest impression on the reader.
- **Step 6** Write the body of your letter, using your outline as a guide. Write two or three short paragraphs that state and explain your facts, in the order you chose. If you are writing a covering letter that goes with a résumé, don't retell what is in your résumé. Focus instead on why you should be the person the company hires. Identify your unique skills and qualities.
- **Step 7** Write a short, closing paragraph for your letter. How you end the letter will depend on why you are writing it, but do include any final information your reader might need. You might want to restate your purpose using other words. Or you might want to thank the reader for considering your request. If you're writing a letter of complaint, tell the reader exactly what you'd like him or her to do to satisfy you.
- **Step 8** Revise the ideas in your letter. Ask yourself: Have I been clear? Have I said everything I need to say? Is there anything that isn't necessary that I should delete? Have I used proper business letter form?
- **Step 9** Edit your work, taking time to check your grammar and spelling carefully. (You might want to use the spell check and grammar check on your computer.) Look for repeated words and use the thesaurus to help you replace them.
- **Step 10** Print or type your letter and sign your name. Make sure your name, address, phone and fax numbers, and e-mail address are on the letter so that you can be contacted.

Making It Work: Writing

Here are three different kinds of formal letters. As you read them, think about why the language used in each one is different.

Model 1

sender's name and address
> LaVerne Watson
> 133 Elm Street
> Dartmouth, NS
> B4L 1B2

date — March 12, 2002

where letter is being sent; name and address
> Mr. N. Ito
> Superior Appliance Repair
> 2700 Wilson Road
> Dartmouth, NS
> B4L 2C3

formal greeting — Dear Mr. Ito,

I am writing this letter to <u>complain about the service</u> I received when — purpose of letter
your company sent a repair person to my home on <u>March 5, 2002</u>. — date of incident

The dispatcher told me that the repair person would arrive between 12:00 and 2:00. At 3:00, I was still waiting. The repair person finally arrived at 3:30. She had a work order that listed the part I needed for my dryer, but she did not have the part with her. She planned to leave, pick up the part, and return the next day. I needed my dryer fixed right away and she could not do that. I was forced to call for after-hours service from another company, who fixed my dryer that night. However, I had to pay an extra $50.00 for the service. — details of incident

I feel that your repair person should have made an effort to return with the part once she knew it was missing. Since she could not,
action that writer wants taken — <u>I would like your company to reimburse me for the $50.00 charge</u> I ended up paying. A copy of the bill is enclosed.

<u>I look forward to hearing from you.</u>

formal closing — Sincerely,

LaVerne Watson

LaVerne Watson

Model 2

sender's name and address:
Michel Lacroix
Box 49
Timmins, Ontario
P4N 1B3

date: November 6, 2002

where letter is being sent; name and address:
Rolande Brown
Quick Cuts
100 Main Street
Timmins, Ontario
P4N 1B5

formal greeting: Dear Mr. Brown,

Please accept my letter of application for the position of hairstylist, which was advertised in the *Era-Banner* on Monday, November 4. — *introductory sentence — purpose of letter*

As you will see from the attached résumé, I have several years of experience in hair salons. I am very friendly and enjoy working with people to make them look and feel good. I learn quickly and am always interested in new experiences. I think you would find me a good addition to your hairstyling team. — *main body of text with relevant information*

I look forward to hearing from you.

formal closing: Sincerely,

Michel Lacroix

Michel Lacroix

Making It Work: Writing

Model 3

sender's name and address
Two Brothers Mechanics
Box 98
Sioux Lookout, ON
P8T 1B7

date — August 27, 2002

where letter is being sent; name and address
Sarah Mason
Mason Auto Parts
1243 Main Street
St. Catharines, ON
L4X 1A2

formal greeting — Dear Ms. Mason,

We have received the shipment of parts ordered from your company on August 1, 2001. All parts ordered were delivered. — **introductory sentence — purpose of letter**

Please find enclosed our cheque in the amount of $4700.00 to cover the invoice included with your delivery.

We look forward to working with you again.

formal closing — Sincerely,

Thomas Silver

TWO BROTHERS MECHANICS

Think about It

What similarities and differences do you see in Models 1, 2, and 3?

Use the Anthology

You can find formal letters on pages 219-220. Do you think those letters show that the steps outlined here were taken to write them? Explain your thinking.

Activities

1. Write a letter of complaint about a real or imagined service you received (bike repair, stereo purchase) that was not satisfactory. Remember that you want to complain, but you also want the service to be completed. Make sure your tone is balanced.

2. Imagined that you have seen a one-week summer cottage rental advertised, and you and a group of friends wish to rent the cottage. Write two letters of inquiry. The first letter should have a familiar tone (you are writing to someone who knows you). The second letter is a formal letter to someone you do not know. Both letters must ask for details about the rental and show that you and your friends are responsible and reliable.

How to Write a Résumé

Before You Start

A résumé is a short, well-organized summary of who you are, what you have done, and what skills you have. There is no right way to write a résumé, but there are three typical styles of résumé writing — a chronological résumé, a functional résumé, and a combination résumé. You'll find models on pages 79-81.

The key to a good résumé is to present your information clearly, concisely, and in an easy-to-read format. The ideal résumé is no longer than two pages. It includes your full name, address, and phone number, and fax number and e-mail address if you have them.

Before you follow the steps to write a résumé, think about these questions:

- Do you already have a résumé? How is it organized?
- What kinds of information have you included in your résumé or have you seen in other résumés?
- If you don't have a résumé, what information might you include when writing one?
- Why do you think it is important to take into account the kind of job you are applying for when deciding what style of résumé to write?

Do It Yourself

Steps

- **Step 1** Decide which of the three kinds of résumés you want to write. The information you need for the résumé will determine the data you need to collect.

- **Step 2** Collect the data you need for your résumé. To do this, look at the information included in sample résumés on pages 79-81. You can also complete a copy of Line Master 3 (from your teacher), and think about the action words below. Some action words essential to a résumé include:

| achieved | answered | assembled | built |
| advised | arranged | began | cared for |

coached	filed	listened	reorganized
completed	gathered	managed	sold
constructed	guided	operated	selected
created	helped	organized	taught
decided	improved	planned	tested
encouraged	instructed	prepared	trained
explained	led	repaired	volunteered

Use the present tense of verbs if they refer to a position you presently hold.

- **Step 3** Begin your résumé with your name, address, phone number, e-mail address, and fax number. You can use a word-processing program to create a letterhead template. Put your name in bold face or large type.

- **Step 4** Write a career- or job-objective statement to make clear the reason you are applying for the job. Some sample job-objective statements are:

    Job Objective: To obtain a summer position doing lawn maintenance and landscaping

    Career Objective: To obtain a full-time position as a server

- **Step 5** Write a list of your skills below your name and address. At a glance, an employer can identify whether or not you have the necessary skills to do the job.

- **Step 6** Complete a first draft of your résumé according to the model you chose.

- **Step 7** Edit and revise your résumé. Have you clearly stated your skills? Have you followed the model to provide all necessary information? Are your name, address, and phone number included?

- **Step 8** Check and correct your grammar and spelling. Have someone you trust, who has good writing skills, proofread it. An employer will often disregard a résumé and covering letter if there is even one typing or spelling error. Complete your final version.

Hot tips

- Repeat your name at the top of each page.
- Single-space your résumé, but include a space between sections.
- Always type your résumé — never write it by hand.
- Use the same font, and paper size (8 1/2 × 11) and colour as your covering letter.
- Avoid brightly coloured paper with fancy, hard-to-read script. Basic colours such as white, off-white, and grey are best.
- Be honest. Do not exaggerate or lie about the skills you possess.
- Do not put your résumé in a binder or folder.
- Do not include irrelevant personal information, such as weight, or height.

On the next pages are samples of each kind of résumé. As you read them, think about how they are similar and how they are different.

Functional résumé

- focus on skills, downplays a lack of experience
- tells where and how skills gained
- evidence of hard work, commitment to a team or volunteer work, good marks at school

This style suits someone looking for a first job.

Model 1

Richard Jones
Box 23
Outlook, Saskatchewan S0L 2K3
Tel: (306) 555-1913
E-mail: rjones@sp.com

SUMMARY OF SKILLS

- Can do many tasks at once — focus on skills
- Committed to seeing things through
- Hardworking and dedicated
- Easily adapts to different environments
- Learns new tasks quickly

SKILLS & EXPERIENCES

General Labour

- Lifted over 30 kg for extended periods of time — tells where and how skills gained
- Operated various types of farm equipment
- Performed building maintenance tasks: roof repair, caulking, eavestrough cleaning
- Did interior and exterior painting

Sales

- Managed table at local farmers' market
- Set wages according to current prices

EDUCATION

1998 to present   Outlook High School
                    Outlook, Saskatchewan (to graduate 2002)

References available upon request

Chronological résumé

- experience listed by date
- résumé divided into sections (work experience, education, volunteer work, achievements and awards)
- most recent job and educational experiences listed first

This style suits someone with many experiences to share and is not recommended for use the first time you look for a job.

Model 2

Jennifer Alderman
63 Westchester Street
Winnipeg, Manitoba R5T 2K4
Tel: (204) 555-4726
Fax: (204) 555-4727

Highlights of Qualifications:

- Hardworking, honest, and reliable
- Experience dealing with children
- Good problem-solving skills
- Can do many things at once
- Good with people

Relevant Experience:

1997–present   **Caregiver, part-time**
               Falcon Family, Winnipeg, MB

- Care for two children under the age of five, without supervision
- Prepare meals and snacks
- Plan activities for children
- Supervise when friends come over to play

1995–1997   **Mother's Helper, part-time**
            Falcon Family, Winnipeg, MB

- Assisted with care of newborn baby — feeding, changing
- Played games with two-year-old while mother rested
- Made sure all toys were put away properly
- Taught two-year-old how to say the alphabet

Education:

1999–present   **Lester B. Pearson Secondary School**
               Winnipeg, MB

- Expected date of graduation: Spring 2004

References available upon request

(résumé divided into sections; experience and education listed by date)

Combination résumé

- organized chronologically and by categories
- also includes skills acquired

This résumé is good for those who have had some, but not much, work experience.

Model 3

William Jackson
41 West Street
Toronto, Ontario M5A 6L3
Tel: (416) 555-9286
E-mail: william.jackson@provider.ca

HIGHLIGHTS OF QUALIFICATIONS OR SUMMARY OF SKILLS

- Trustworthy, responsible, reliable
- Works well with others or independently
- Able to complete tasks within limited time
- Committed employee
- Experience handling cash and cheque transactions
- Able to use a variety of landscaping equipment responsibly and safely

organized in sections

RELEVANT SKILLS AND ABILITIES

General Labour

- Operated gas-powered lawn mower and trimmer
- Loaded and unloaded equipment from truck
- Worked over sixty hours a week and maintained productivity
- Hauled away trimmings and debris

Customer Service

- Maintained good relationships with clients by always being friendly and polite
- Helped company grow by asking clients for referrals
- Collected payments and issued receipts
- Called clients to verify that rain dates were convenient

WORK HISTORY

1998 to 1999	Landscaper	Grasscutters	Toronto
1997 to 1998	Landscaper	J & T Landscaping	Toronto

organized chronologically

EDUCATION

1999	Diploma	MacDonald Secondary School	Toronto

References available upon request

Think about It

Which of these résumés most appeals to you? Why?

Use the Anthology

Look at the résumé on page 90 of the anthology. What can you tell about the writer of the résumé?

Activities

1. Create a résumé that you could use to apply for a part-time summer job.

2. Create a list of questions that you could ask a partner to find out about his or her work history, hobbies, and personal attributes. Next, find a partner and ask him or her the questions. Then read that person's résumé. Does the résumé give the same impression as the interview did? Switch roles and repeat the activity.

How to Write a Covering Letter

Before You Start

A covering letter is a short, formal letter to go with your résumé. It tells the employer about the qualities that you have, and gives information about you as a worker that does not appear in your résumé.

A covering letter gives you the opportunity to give a good impression and let the employer know that:

— you're the best person for the job
— you can do the job
— you want the job
— you have special skills

Before you follow the steps to write a covering letter, think about these questions:

- Have you ever written a covering letter? Do you think it was effective? Why or why not?
- Employers usually scan a covering letter very quickly. What information do you want an employer to know about you right away?
- What words might you use to give an employer a positive impression of you?

Do It Yourself

Step 1 Decide what information needs to go in your letter, based on the situation. You might be answering a job ad, or you might be submitting a résumé to a place where you want to work.

If you are answering a job ad, read the ad carefully. Look for words that show what the employer wants in an employee ("Our company is looking for skilled workers who demonstrate a strong work ethic and are willing to …"). Make a list of those skills or attributes, then make notes about how you can demonstrate them.

If you are applying for a job at a place where you want to work, or answering an ad that doesn't describe exact qualities, think about the skills that you think most employers look for in potential employees (hard working, honest, gets along well with others, willing to try new things, takes the initiative, and so on). List as many as you can. Then pick two or three and make notes about how you demonstrate them.

Charts like these can help you identify your skills from past and current jobs and see how well your skills match with the ones an employer wants.

JOB CHART

Work Experience	Responsibilities
Cashier	handled cash
	communicated with customers
	was familiar with stock
Paper route	handled money
	carried heavy bag with papers
	woke up early to complete route
Volunteer treasurer, hockey team	handled money
	communicated with team members and their families
	operated team bank account

SKILLS CHART

Employer wants:	I:
Strong work ethic	• have excellent attendance at school
	• was involved in sports and other extra-curricular activities and still maintained good marks
	• never missed assigned dates when volunteering

Outgoing, pleasant personality	• can get reference letter from a teacher or administrator at school to support my statement that I have this quality • can list the jobs and volunteer positions where I've worked with others (seniors, young people, peers, adults)
Good computer skills	• can identify the level at which I use computers • can list on my résumé computer programs that I can use • can stress my willingness to learn

- **Step 2** Look at your information and decide on the order in which you want to present it.

    Most often, you will state how you learned about the job (from an ad, from a sign in a window, or simply that you like the workplace and would like to work there). Next, you will describe how you demonstrate the skills or attitudes the employer wants. Next, make a statement that summarizes what you have said in your letter. Finally, end with a statement that tells an employer when, where, and how to reach you.

- **Step 3** Write a first draft of your letter. When you are finished, check the ad again. How does the employer want to receive applications? Follow the directions given. If the employer wants applications by e-mail and you don't have a computer, ask a friend for the use of a computer, use your school computer, or use a computer at the local library.

- **Step 4** Prepare your final draft in block style or modified block style, using the model on page 87 as a guide. Include your personal information (name, address, phone number, fax number, e-mail address), the date, and the employer's information (hiring manager's name and title, company's name and address). Check and correct your grammar and your spelling.

Hot tips

- Direct your letter to a specific person. An ad will often indicate a hiring manager. If it doesn't, call the company and ask for the name of the person who will be hiring for the position.
- Use plain white, off-white, or light grey 8 1/2 x 11 paper.
- Type your covering letter.
- Use the same font and style as your résumé.
- Single-space the covering letter, but double-space between paragraphs.
- Covering letters are especially important when applying for an entry-level full-time or part-time job.
- Write a covering letter when applying for a job that has an application form. This may give you an edge over other applicants.
- Do not use the same covering letter for every job. Change the letter to fit each job. This may take minor adjustments but it shows the employer you understand the particular requirements of the job for which you are applying.
- Avoid overusing the word "I."
- If you leave a phone number, you might want to have an answering machine on that phone line. Be sure your recording sounds professional.
- Do not enclose a photo unless it is requested or you are an actor.

How to Write a Covering Letter

Here is a covering letter. Read it and think about the things you notice that make it similar or different from other letters you have read.

Model

your name and address:

Emma Cho
4667–413 22nd Ave.
Edmonton, AB T6K 1Z2
(403) 555-7890
Emma@theweb.ca

letter is set in modified block-style format (all information begins at left; sender's information is set as letterhead)

date: January 26, 2003

employer's information:
Dr. Eva Night
2 South St.
Edmonton, AB T5L 4A3

name of person who is hiring:
Dear Dr. Night:

At Scott Smith's last appointment, you mentioned that you would be needing some extra reception help in your office soon. My friend Scott was kind enough to pass this information on to me. If this is still the case, I would like to offer my services.

Paragraph 1 — introductory statement — includes the position for which you are applying and how you heard about the position

Paragraph 2 — convincing details that show you are the best candidate – discuss your skills, identify the characteristics that you have which make you the best choice for the job, do not retell employment history that is in your résumé

For the past three months, I have been working part time, three evenings per week, as a telemarketer at ABC Corp., downtown. Talking with up to 50 customers per evening, I have gained a great deal of customer service experience. I am confident on the phone and I also have basic computer skills.

Attached is my résumé. I would be available to work part time on weekdays. I have always thought of doctors' offices as friendly environments and so I know I would enjoy working with you. Please contact me at the phone number above during regular office hours. I hope to hear from you soon.

Paragraph 3 — concluding statement – where, when, and how you can be reached for an interview

Sincerely,

Emma Cho

sign in blue or black ink

Emma Cho

Think about It

Find examples of word choice that help to create the letter's assertive tone. What makes this tone so effective in a cover letter?

Use the Anthology

You'll find another covering letter on page 89 of the anthology. How does it compare to the one you read here?

Activities

1. a. From the newspaper, choose an ad for a job that interests you. Write a covering letter to accompany your résumé for this job.

   b. Work with a partner. Exchange covering letters. Read one another's letters and decide if you would consider interviewing this person for a job. Discuss your reasons for your choice with your partner. Based on the covering letter, what are the person's strengths? How could the person's letter be improved?

How to Write and Send E-mail

Before You Start

Electronic mail, or e-mail, is a service that lets you send and receive mail, anywhere in the world, on a computer. E-mail is fast and can be a great way to keep in touch with family and friends. It is also an excellent way to communicate for business purposes. Companies may ask for your e-mail address so they can respond to your application. In many cases, companies will only accept applications through e-mail. Your response helps them see how comfortable you are with technology.

Before you follow the steps to write and send an e-mail message, think about these questions:
- Do you already use e-mail? Do you like using it or not? Explain.
- What do you use e-mail for right now?
- What other uses for e-mail do you think you might have in the next few years?

Do It Yourself

Step 1 Before you send e-mail, you need an e-mail address. E-mail addresses have two parts, separated by an @ (you read this aloud as "at.") An example is Me@home.com. Before the @ is the mailbox, which is your name. After the @ is the domain, which is usually the name of your Internet service provider. In the workplace, your employer may provide you with an e-mail address. Outside of the workplace, you may have access to a computer at school, at the local library, or at home. You can get free, Web-based e-mail from a provider such as Hotmail, Yahoo, or msn.

To sign up for a free e-mail address, go to the provider's Web site (Hotmail: www.hotmail.com; Yahoo: www.yahoo.ca; msn: www.msn.com). Each will take you, step by step, through the process of setting up an e-mail address.

Step 2 Access your e-mail through the Web browser when you turn on your computer.

- **Step 3** Follow the provider's instructions for beginning a new message. Type the address of the person you are e-mailing in the "To" field. Type the subject in the "Subject" field. If you want to send the same message to other people, fill in the "Cc" field.

- **Step 4** Write your message. Use the spell-check, dictionary, or thesaurus functions to help make your writing clear and correct.

- **Step 5** Click on "Send," or follow the provider's instructions, when you are ready to send your message.

- **Step 6** To check your messages, access your e-mail account when you turn on your computer. Follow the directions to get to your in-box, which will have a list of your new messages.

HOT tips

- Your employer has the right to track your e-mail use at the office. Be sure to follow any rules your workplace has about e-mail.
- All e-mail can be traced. Make sure the content of your messages is appropriate, and think carefully about what you're sending and to whom you are sending it.
- There are rules of politeness, or etiquette, to follow when writing e-mails. You can find a book in the library or do an online search for e-mail etiquette.

On the next page is an e-mail message. How is it different from other kinds of messages, for example, quick notes, formal letters, phone messages?

How to Write and Send E-mail

Model

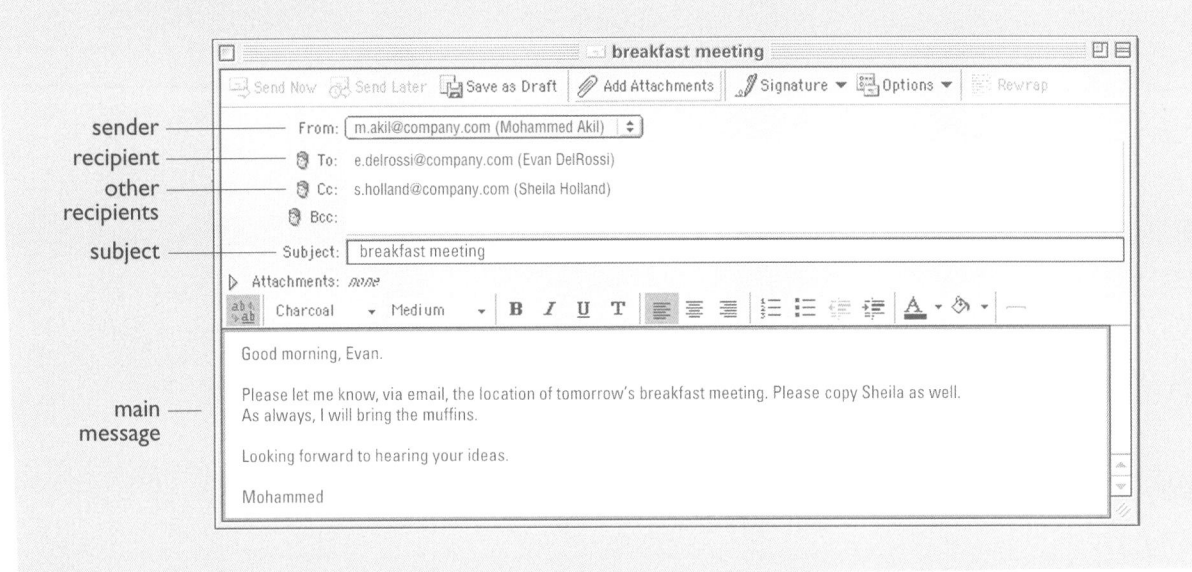

sender — From: m.akil@company.com (Mohammed Akil)
recipient — To: e.delrossi@company.com (Evan DelRossi)
other recipients — Cc: s.holland@company.com (Sheila Holland)
Bcc:
subject — Subject: breakfast meeting
Attachments: none

main message —
Good morning, Evan.

Please let me know, via email, the location of tomorrow's breakfast meeting. Please copy Sheila as well. As always, I will bring the muffins.

Looking forward to hearing your ideas.

Mohammed

Think about It

An e-mail message should still follow the basic format of a letter. Look at the model and outline that basic format.

Use the Anthology

There are e-mail messages on page 221. What characteristics of the model above do you see in the e-mail messages in the anthology?

Activities

1. Set up a free e-mail address. Send e-mails to at least three of your classmates. How is the tone of a personal e-mail different from one that you might write in the workplace?

2. Write, but don't send, an e-mail in response to a job advertisement from the student anthology, the newspaper, or an Internet job site. How is the e-mail you wrote different from a letter you might write responding to the same job? How is it similar?

Language

TABLE OF CONTENTS

Using Language	94
How to Follow Oral Instructions	98
How to Identify the Main Idea while Listening	102
How to Create and Present an Oral Summary	105
How to Choose a Graphic Organizer to Summarize Discussion	110
How to Be an Effective Group Member	113
How to Complete Work in Groups	117
How to Create a Personal Dictionary	121
How to Build a Specialized Vocabulary	124
How to Create a Personal Style Guide	128
How to Choose Appropriate Language	132
How to Make a Presentation	136
How to Conduct an Interview	141

Using Language

First impressions count, both in the workplace and beyond. To make a good first impression, you need to know how to use language well. Being able to choose the right words for each situation is an important skill for success in life.

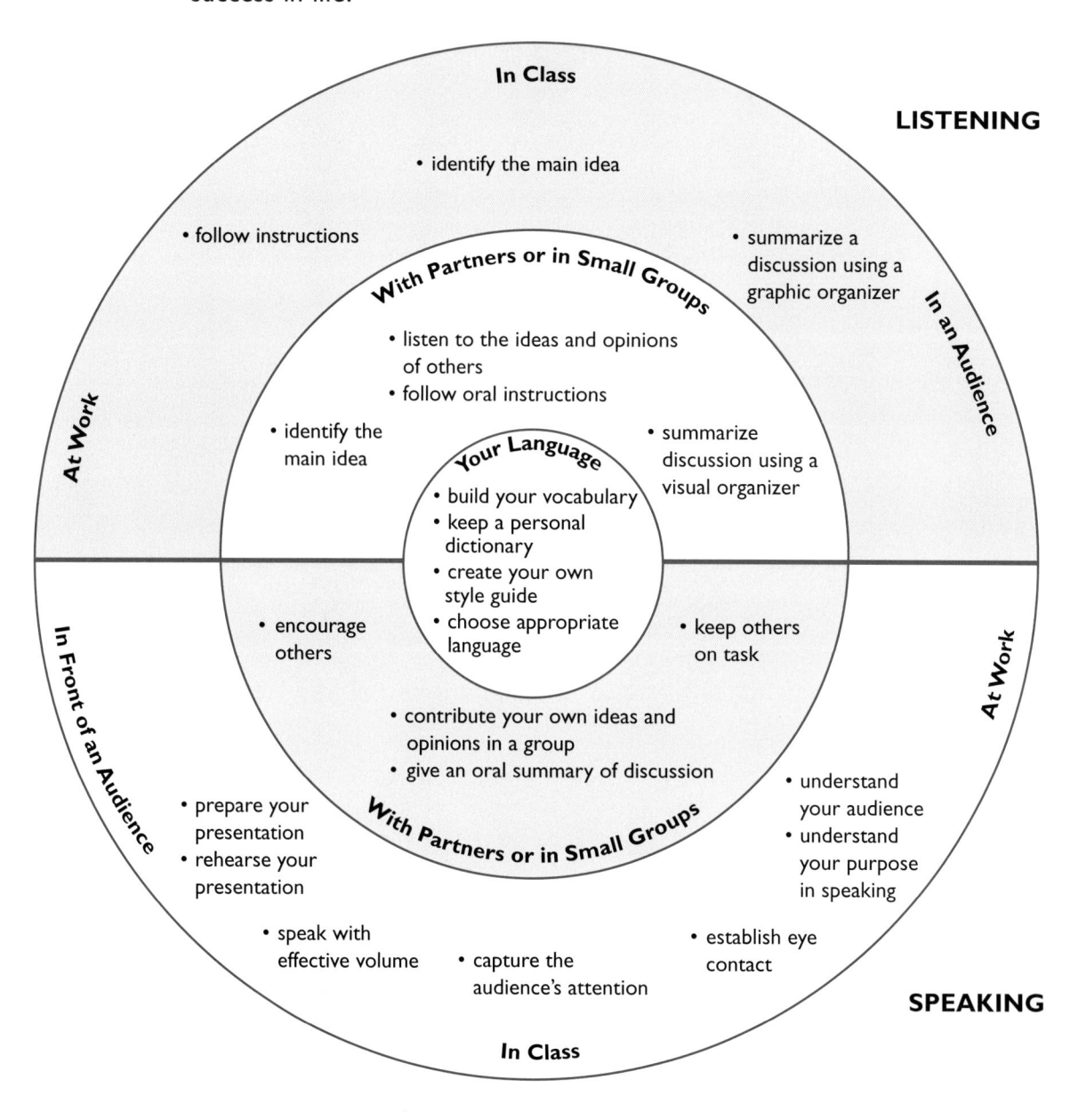

LISTENING

In Class
- identify the main idea
- summarize a discussion using a graphic organizer

At Work
- follow instructions

With Partners or in Small Groups
- listen to the ideas and opinions of others
- follow oral instructions
- identify the main idea

In an Audience
- summarize discussion using a visual organizer

Your Language
- build your vocabulary
- keep a personal dictionary
- create your own style guide
- choose appropriate language

SPEAKING

With Partners or in Small Groups
- encourage others
- keep others on task
- contribute your own ideas and opinions in a group
- give an oral summary of discussion

In Front of an Audience
- prepare your presentation
- rehearse your presentation

At Work
- understand your audience
- understand your purpose in speaking

In Class
- speak with effective volume
- capture the audience's attention
- establish eye contact

Listening, speaking, and working in groups are all important parts of using language. The questions on the next few pages can help you understand how well you do each language task. Copy each list of questions into your notebook. Beside each item on the list, answer whether you do the skill quite well, well, well enough, or not very well. Answer the quizzes several times during the year to see how your language skills are changing.

▸ Listening is a critical skill

Employers say that being a good listener is one of the key skills their employees need. A good listener knows what his or her tasks are and can do work completely and accurately.

At school, being a good listener means that you can understand instructions and know what you're expected to do. You can ask for clarification if there's something you don't understand. Hearing and thinking about other people's opinions helps you grow in knowledge and understanding.

Being a good listener is most important in your personal relationships. It is a skill that is vital to solid friendships and partnerships throughout your life. Answer these questions to learn how good a listener you are.

Your listening skills

How effectively do you:

1. follow instructions that are given to you orally?
2. summarize (orally) what you have heard?
3. identify the main idea in what you've heard?
4. use visual or graphic organizers to record and summarize what you've heard?
5. listen to the opinions of others in groups?

▸ Being a good speaker

Ever since you said your first word, you have been sharing your thoughts, feelings, and observations with the people around you. Being able to speak and use language makes humans different from all other animals. We can share what is inside us with other people; they can know us and we can know them.

Whether you are speaking to one person, a small group, or a large group, you will help others know and understand you through your speaking skills. Answer these questions to learn how effective a speaker you are.

Your speaking skills

How effectively do you:

1. prepare your presentation?
2. rehearse your presentation?
3. keep the audience interested in what you're saying?

4. speak naturally, using your notes but not always reading from them?
5. keep an effective volume while you're speaking?
6. make eye contact (if appropriate) with the audience?
7. use the right words and phrases that suit the audience and your purpose in speaking?
8. use the appropriate tone for your purpose and audience?

▸ Working well in a group

In many jobs, employees need to work with others to understand issues, solve problems, and create products of various kinds. It can be difficult to work with others. If you can work well with many types of people — even those you may not like — you will be on the road to success in the workforce.

Working in a group is a challenge, but it is worth that challenge for the higher-quality work and results that usually come out of group work. Answer these questions to learn how well you work in a group.

Your group skills

How effectively do you:

1. keep a positive attitude toward group work?
2. come prepared with what you need to work with the group?
3. get along with others to complete a task?
4. do your part to get the work done, but not do the work that others should do?
5. keep the group on task?
6. listen to the opinions of others in groups?
7. contribute your own ideas in groups?
8. help others without doing their work for them?

How to Follow Oral Instructions

Before You Start

To follow instructions — at school, at home, and in the workplace — we have to understand the task and remember its steps in order.

Before you take the steps to following oral instructions, think about these questions:

- What types of oral instructions do you receive at home, at school, or at work?
- When do you find instructions easy to follow? Why? When do you find them challenging to follow? Why?

Do It Yourself

Step 1 Listen carefully to the instructions you are given.

Step 2 Make sure you understand the end result of your specific task. Confirm your understanding with the person who gave the task by repeating it ("So, I'm supposed to make 12 copies of this document, collate them, and staple them. You need these on your desk by 1:00. Correct?")

Step 3 Make sure you understand the steps you need to follow, and the order of the steps. Using one or more of these strategies can help.

> **Verbal rehearsal** — Rehearse the steps verbally, repeating all of the steps in order after they have been given.
>
> **Visualization** — In your mind, see yourself doing each step as the instruction is given.
>
> **Written instructions** — For a task with many steps, or one you haven't done before, write down each step as the instructions are given, then read the list back right away to confirm. Consult your list and follow it as you work. Check off each step as you complete it.

How to Follow Oral Instructions | 99

Instruction manual — For a task that requires you to use a new piece of equipment or technology, ask to read the manual so that you can use the tool confidently to complete the task.

Step 4 Complete the task. When you're finished, review the steps that you used, either aloud or in your mind. Make sure you have followed all the steps and completed the whole task.

Hot tips

- Ask questions. Asking questions shows that you are thoughtful and care about doing the job correctly.

Rajiv is in a co-op placement at a large retail firm, working as a buyer's assistant. The buyer wants Rajiv to call a supplier to find a missing shipment. What do you notice about the language the buyer uses?

Model

Rajiv, one of your jobs here will be to call suppliers to track down missing shipments. The manager at the Guelph store just called to say that she hasn't received her perfume shipment yet from Ace Cosmetics, and she needs it by Friday. Here's the purchase order number and the date it was ordered. Call the supplier and ask to speak to the distribution manager. Give him or her this information, and ask who the shipper was, the bill of lading number, and the shipment date. Then call the store with the information. Any questions?

- indicates Rajiv will need to use this process again ("Rajiv, one of your jobs here")
- situation to be resolved ("just called to... yet from Ace")
- buyer's instructions ("Call the supplier and ask to speak to the distribution manager.")
- what Rajiv should do/say/ask
- opportunity to ask questions ("Any questions?")

Think about It

If you were Rajiv, what would you do to be sure that you understood your supervisor's instructions?

Use the Anthology

Read How to Assemble Your Fax Machine on pages 141–143. If you were given those instructions orally, what strategies might help you remember them? What else might help you remember those instructions?

Activities

1. One way to keep track of instructions, especially complicated ones, is to use a flowchart to outline the steps. The advantage of a flowchart is that it lets you follow different sets of instructions depending on the situation. Read this flowchart. On a separate sheet of paper, record the steps Rajiv should take if the parcel has been shipped, and the steps he should take if it has not been shipped.

Get the phone number for the supplier.
↓
Ask to speak to the distribution manager.
↓
Give the distribution manager the purchase order number and order date.
↙   ↘
If the parcel has been shipped: If the parcel has not been shipped:
↓   ↓

Call the store manager and give her the information.

2. Work with a partner to practise following oral instructions. Decide which of you will be partner A and which will be partner B. Each of you will follow the other's instructions for writing something.

Step 1
- Partner B: Close your book. Place a blank sheet of paper in front of you. Prepare to write, following your partner's instructions
- Partner A: Turn to page 70, Step 1, and read to yourself the instructions for setting up a formal letter.

Step 2
- Partner A: Give oral instructions to Partner B about how to set up a formal letter. Partner B should use his or her own home address as the sender's address, and the school address as the recipient's address.
- Partner B: Follow Partner A's instructions on your blank sheet of paper.

Step 3 Together, examine how well B followed A's instructions.

Step 4 Trade roles. Partner B will give Partner A oral instructions about a different writing task from the handbook (such as Steps 3, 4, and 5 of How to Write a Résumé, page 77).

How to Identify the Main Idea while Listening

Before You Start

It's important to know how to sort the main idea from unimportant details when people are talking to you.

Before you follow the steps to identifying the main idea while listening, think about these questions:
- How good a listener do you think you are?
- What can you do to become a better listener?

Do It Yourself

Steps

- **Step 1** Always listen with purpose. Ask yourself:
  What do I need to know?
  What do I think the speaker will say?
  Why is it important to listen to this?

- **Step 2** Listen for the first thing the speaker says. It's important and will give you the focus of the discussion. Keep the topic in mind as you listen. Ask yourself:
  What is the speaker's purpose?
  What should I listen for?

- **Step 3** Look and listen for the speaker's signals.

  Listen to the key words and phrases. Often a speaker will signal to the listener what is important by using such words and phrases as: "The three main points are …" "It's important that …" "What you need to know about this is …."

  Listen to changes in the speaker's volume and tone. Speakers may speak more loudly, distinctly, slowly, or emphatically when they have something important to say.

  Watch the speaker carefully for changes in facial expression or gestures that show that an important or key point is being made.

How to Identify the Main Idea while Listening

> **Use memory aids** while you listen. If the speaker announces that s/he will make three key points, repeat each to yourself after you hear it, count them to yourself, or take brief notes about each one.
>
> ● **Step 4** Once the speaker has finished, repeat the main points to yourself in your head, or write them down on paper.

HOT tips
- Remember that some speakers may be less clear than others. Listen carefully, and ask questions if you need to.
- While the speaker is talking, try to focus only on the speaker.

This is a speech that is meant to be read aloud. While you read it, think about what you would emphasize orally if you were giving this speech to a group.

Model

key phrases — Here are the three worst things to do if you want to be successful in a job interview:

one of the three important points — Don't Show Up on Time. If you're not on time, you'll send your prospective employer the message that you're not organized, and might show up late for work. Being on time is crucial to making a good first impression, because that's the good employee's first rule: be on time.

Just Wear Any Old Thing. If you don't take care with how you're dressed, your employer will think that you don't care about yourself. And if you don't care about yourself, you probably won't care about your work. Wear something that makes you feel confident and says something special about you.

one of the three important points — Don't Have Anything Good to Say About Yourself. If you're not prepared to tell an employer what you're good at, the employer will give the job to someone who is. Don't rely on your résumé to do the job of selling your skills. Come prepared to tell the employer that you're skilled and knowledgeable.

speaker re-states key points — So don't make those three mistakes! Instead, be on time, dress confidently, and tell the employer that you're skilled and knowledgeable.

Think about It

What key words or phrases in the speech help you find the main ideas?

Use the Anthology

Ask a partner to read aloud "Why Idalécio's as Canadian as maple syrup" (pages 30-31). Identify the main ideas while you listen.

Activities

1. Using the model, try a listening exercise with a partner. While one partner reads, the other listens to identify the main ideas. (The reader should use gestures, tone, and volume changes to signal the main ideas to the listener.) Then the listener repeats the main ideas to the reader. Switch places and repeat the exercise.

2. Consider a class at school in which you have particular trouble paying attention. List some things you could do to help you as you listen. Then, in a helpful and respectful tone, list some things that your teacher could do to help you notice the main points more clearly.

How to Create and Present an Oral Summary

Before You Start

A summary gives the main ideas and some key details of a much longer piece of writing, a media experience (a film, video, or audio event), a lecture, a lesson, or a discussion. You may be asked to give an oral summary of something you've read, seen, heard, or discussed. Sometimes these summaries can be delivered in a few sentences. At other times, your oral summary will be longer. Whether it's long or short, it's important that your summary be complete, accurate, and clear.

Before you follow the steps for creating and presenting an effective oral summary, think about these questions:
- Why is it useful to summarize information?
- What do you think is different about a written summary and an oral summary?

Do It Yourself

Steps

- **Step 1** View or read the item you will be summarizing.

- **Step 2** Make notes about what you saw or read, and what information you will need to include in your summary. Use your own words. Organize the main ideas and key details in point form, or use a visual or graphic organizer (see models on pages 106-107 or on Line Master 4, available from your teacher.)

  For informational texts or media, use an organizer that matches your topic. For example, if you're going to give an oral summary of a documentary about the causes of anorexia, use a cause and effect organizer.

  For stories, use a type of story chart to organize the main details of the character, conflict, plot, setting, and theme (see Line Master 5, available from your teacher).

- **Step 3** Write your summary from your notes and any organizers you used.

Step 4 Present your summary orally, but try not to read it directly. Instead, use your notes and any organizers to guide your memory of the details as you speak. Begin by telling your audience the purpose of your summary. Use the framework of your notes or organizer to give order to your thoughts and ideas. Present each main idea in its own sentence.

Hot tips
- Keep your points short and simple.
- Number your points to keep yourself organized.
- Highlight key ideas in colour so that you will see them quickly and easily as you present your summary.

Here are two ways to organize the notes you take as you view, listen, read, or discuss. Which way helps you understand best? Why?

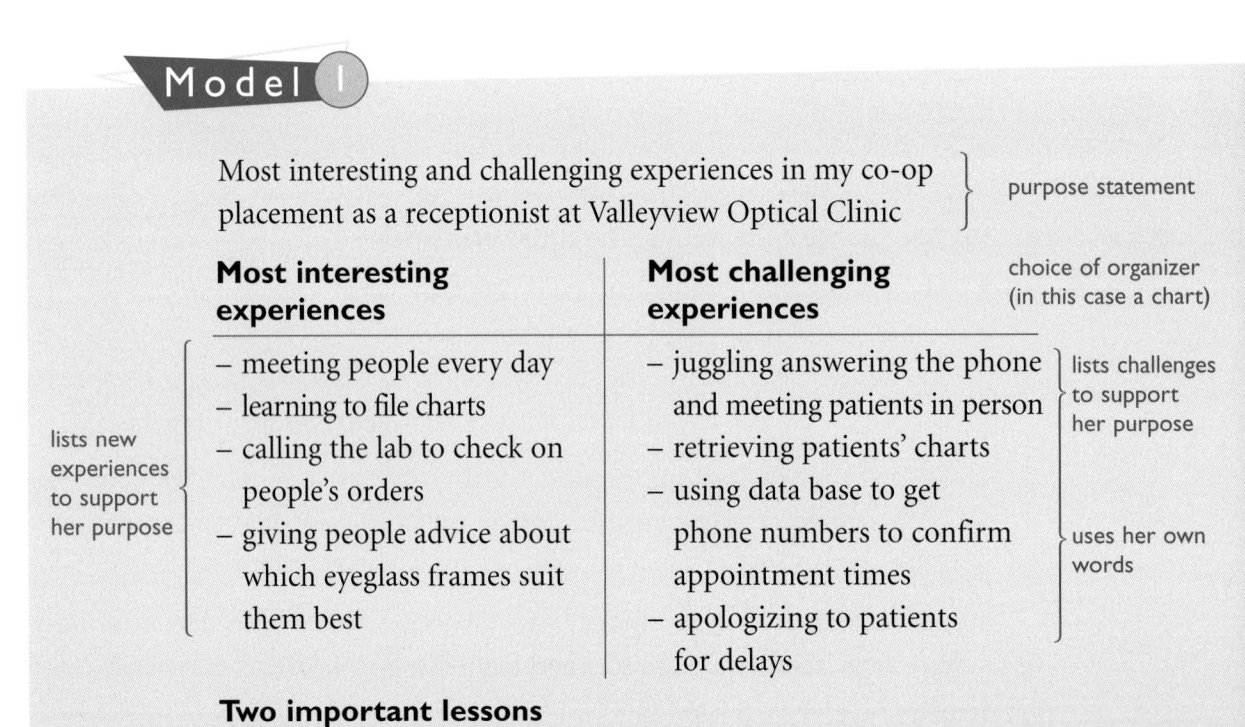

Model 1

Most interesting and challenging experiences in my co-op placement as a receptionist at Valleyview Optical Clinic — *purpose statement*

choice of organizer (in this case a chart)

Most interesting experiences	Most challenging experiences
– meeting people every day – learning to file charts – calling the lab to check on people's orders – giving people advice about which eyeglass frames suit them best	– juggling answering the phone and meeting patients in person – retrieving patients' charts – using data base to get phone numbers to confirm appointment times – apologizing to patients for delays

lists new experiences to support her purpose

lists challenges to support her purpose

uses her own words

Two important lessons

Always be friendly and helpful to patients and staff. — *summation statements*
Always write down instructions for new tasks.

Model 2

Partial Notes for an Oral Summary of a Film — purpose statement
Film: The Great Gatsby — story name
Setting: Long Island, New York, and New York City, 1922 — setting

Main characters	Physical qualities	Personality traits
Jay Gatsby — a mysterious millionaire, owns a huge mansion on Long Island	young, tall, handsome, elegant-looking, well-dressed	mysterious, dreamlike, open, easy-going, rich, doesn't always tell the truth
Daisy Buchanan — Tom's wife, a wealthy socialite	blonde, beautiful, breathy voice, tall	aimless, rich, sophisticated, cynical, a little bit lost and weak
Tom Buchanan — Daisy's husband; has inherited piles of money	brutish, hulking, handsome in a rough way	incredibly rich, prejudiced, boorish, arrogant, pushy

— chart of characters

Story Sequence:

First, we are shown the end of the story: Gatsby dies while he is floating in his pool. Someone has shot him.

Next: the flashback. Summer of 1922. Nick moves to New York.
- is invited to lunch at the Buchanan's
- learns that Tom has a mistress in New York City and that Daisy is unhappy
- Gatsby's name is mentioned and it seems to mean something to Daisy

Then, Nick meets Gatsby. Gatsby invites him to a wild party that goes on all night.

After that, Nick finds out that Gatsby and Daisy were in love before the war.

— sequence of events

Making It Work: Language

sequence of events
- Gatsby has been waiting to meet Daisy again for five years and still loves her
- asks Nick to invite Daisy over
- Gatsby and Daisy fall in love all over again. For Gatsby, it's just like the past. They have an affair.

conflict

Main conflict(s):
- Gatsby wants Daisy to love him just like in the past and say she never loved Tom
- Daisy is unhappy with Tom but can't say she didn't love him

How the conflict is solved:
- Daisy stays with Tom
- Gatsby gets murdered by Wilson

consequences

Consequences for the main characters:
- Gatsby is dead
- Daisy and Tom leave town and don't even come to Gatsby's funeral

summary in own words

What this story says about human nature or about life (theme):
- It's important to have dreams, but sometimes other people can't live up to our expectations of them, so our dreams die

Think about It

Explain how each of the above ways of organizing a summary helps the presenter summarize the important information for the audience. Is each way helpful?

Use the Anthology

Create an oral summary of the main ideas in "The Seven Habits of Highly Effective People" (pages 61-64).

Activities

1. Practise giving an oral summary to a partner using one of the models.
2. Using a story summary style similar to model 2, present an oral summary of a film you've seen or a story you've read.

How to Choose a Graphic Organizer to Summarize Discussion

Before You Start

A summary brings together all the points in a reading or discussion. Some summaries are presented in paragraphs, but they can also be presented in point form, visual formats, or orally. After a group discussion, a summary can help members to recall discussion and decisions as the group works toward its goal.

Graphic/visual organizers help you to note the main points of discussion, and they also help you to organize and connect the ideas in an easy-to-read format.

Before you follow these steps to choose a visual organizer, think about these questions:
- When else do you think visual organizers would be helpful?
- In which of your school subjects do you use visual/graphic organizers regularly? How does it help?

Do It Yourself

Steps

- **Step 1** Think about the kind of work — the thinking and problem-solving — your group is doing. Then listen to and think about to the kinds of words you will hear in your group. Choose an organizer based on those words (see Line Master 4, available from your teacher):

    When you are generating ideas ("that reminds me," "I remember," "I think"), use brainstorming lists, semantic maps, and thought webs.

    When you are making comparisons ("same," "different," "like," "unlike," "compared to"), use Venn diagrams and compare/contrast charts.

    When you are linking cause and effect ("causes," "as a result," "because, since"), use cause/effect diagrams and fishbone diagrams.

    When you are showing order ("first," "second," "third," "next," "then," "after," "before," "last," "at last," "now," "tomorrow"), use timelines, chronology charts, and sequence charts.

When you are drawing conclusions ("therefore," "so," "thus," "it follows that," "as a result," "then"), conclusions diagrams and arch diagrams are good organizers

When you are making decisions based on possible outcomes ("if", "then," "so," "next," "step one," "step two"), use flow chart diagrams.

Step 2 Once you have chosen your organizer, fit your group's ideas into the structure of the organizer.

H●T tips

- Take time before your group begins its discussion to decide together which graphic organizer to use.
- Choose two people to be note-takers for the group (especially if the group is large). One note-taker may have included information that the other didn't.
- Leave five minutes at the end of the discussion for the note-taker to read back the recorded ideas to the group so that you can add, delete, or change ideas.

Here are a few minutes of dialogue from a group discussion. The group is making a plan for designing and producing a travel brochure. What kinds of organizing words are the groups members using?

Model

Sanjay: I think the <u>first</u> thing we should do is to decide the <u>order</u> and who's doing what. That okay?

Dora: Good idea. Since it was my idea to choose Fiji as our destination, I'll go get the information on it.

Lin: <u>Where</u> will you look?

Dora: I'll ask the Librarian, but if he's busy, I'll go to the Internet — probably during lunch <u>next period</u>. So I think I'll be able to have some printouts for us to use <u>tomorrow</u>.

> **Lin:** I've got a few travel brochures at home. They're for the Caribbean, I think. I'll bring them tomorrow so we can decide on a format.
>
> **Sanjay:** That might be a lot to do tomorrow. We've got <u>five days</u> to have it ready. We should plan what we're going to do <u>each day</u>. What information do we need?
>
> **Lin:** Let's check our notes and see what information needs to be in a travel brochure. Then Dora'll know what she needs to find out.
>
> **Dora:** Great! Let's do that <u>now</u>.

Think about It

The key words in the model all relate to time order and decision-making. What possible visual/graphic organizers could the group use to help make its plan?

Use the Anthology

Read "The Canadian Code of Advertising Standards" (pages 117-119). Choose an appropriate visual/graphic organizer to summarize your discussion of this document.

Activities

1. Using group work that you are doing in any of your classes, choose the appropriate graphic organizer to summarize your group discussions. Explain why you think it is the appropriate organizer, and what signal words helped you decide. Use the organizer to summarize one of your group's discussions.

2. Choose two of the visual/graphic organizers. For each, write an appropriate workplace group discussion scenario.

How to Be an Effective Group Member

Before You Start

One of the most important skills you need is the ability to work in a group to get things done. You want to be the kind of person that others want to work with and can rely on. Effective group members:
- arrive at the group prepared to work
- are good listeners
- keep themselves on task
- contribute ideas and encourage others to listen to all ideas
- do their own part, (not everyone else's)
- are reliable
- are flexible
- set both personal and group goals.

Before you follow these steps to being an effective group member, think about these questions:
- What positive things do you contribute when you work in a group?
- What do you think you could improve about your work in a group?

Do It Yourself

Step 1 Bring all notes, books, and materials that you and your group need to complete your task. Keep a positive attitude.

Step 2 Show that you are listening by:
- looking at the speaker
- leaning toward the speaker
- being respectful and not talking or doing other work
- nodding when you agree, or saying so
- asking good questions when a speaker is finished

Step 3 Keep yourself and your group on track by:
- reminding yourself and others of the purpose of the group work when the discussion becomes unfocussed

- politely reminding others to return to the topic
- helping the group to set goals for each group work meeting
- watching the time

Step 4 Keep the discussion going, and keep it positive, by:
- helping the group set an order or rules for speaking
- disagreeing with others in an agreeable way ("That's a good point. I think...")
- using polite gestures, such as putting up your hand, to attract the attention of group members
- speaking in turn
- asking others for their opinions

Step 5 Take responsibility for your own work in the group by:
- knowing the group's goals
- reminding yourself of your own strengths
- volunteering to do things you know you can do
- encouraging other people to do their best
- listening to what others want to do
- helping to set deadlines that everyone can meet

Step 6 Be reliable by:
- showing up for meetings on time
- keeping your word about what you've agreed to
- contacting someone in the group ahead of time if you will be absent

Step 7 Set goals, and give yourself and the group credit when you achieve them.

Hot tips

- Try to keep your group to a maximum of four people. With more than four people you can spread out the workload, but you may find it harder to stay focussed.

How to Be an Effective Group Member | 115

The following is an example of what might happen when people work in a group. As you read, think about the positive and negative behaviours described.

Model

Alicia is having some trouble working in a group. It's getting to the point that no one wants Alicia to be in their group anymore. Her friends know that she is a very interesting and creative person and could potentially do really good work, but they don't know how to make it happen.

Alicia has been assigned to a group in her culinary arts class. There are five people in the group, including Alicia. Their job is to choose the cuisine of a country of their choice and to design and produce a menu for a five-course dinner. The group has four class periods to make decisions, do research, and design and produce the menu.

showing up late takes time from the group when the task has to be explained again

Alicia was there on the first day, but she was twenty minutes late. Group members had to explain the assignment to Alicia, then Alicia didn't really pay attention to what the group was doing. She pretended to listen but she was using the class time to finish her math homework instead. The group decided, without Alicia's input, to design a menu of Thai food. Near the end of the class, the group asked Alicia if she'd go to the library after school to print out some information on Thai soups. Alicia agreed.

not being focussed means you can't help do the work

The next day, Alicia was late again. She hadn't done the research, and she spent the rest of the period walking around talking to members of other groups. Her group planned the rest of the menu, and decided to give Alicia another chance. They made her promise that she'd find a soup recipe to bring to the next class. Alicia promised that she would.

not showing up to meetings means more work for others

Alicia did not come to the next class (day three of the assignment). Another person in the group had to do Alicia's research for her.

Alicia arrived in class on time on the last day of the assignment (day four). She was very interested in the design of the menu booklet and spent the whole period working on it. She volunteered to take it home to finish the final copy for the group, but the group didn't trust her to finish it or to come to class the next day. They did want Alicia's help, however, so they all agreed to meet after school to finish it. Alicia didn't make it to this after-school meeting, so the group finished the booklet without her.

poor group behaviour means people learn not to trust you

Think about It

What positive things did the group do to include Alicia? What do you think Alicia's biggest problem is? What advice would you give her about how to improve?

Use the Anthology

In "Teach Me the Ways of the Sacred Circle" (pages 6-20), Elaine, Matt, and Sam work well as a group. What are some of the reasons for their success? When they have problems, how do they solve them?

Activities

1. Think of a group with which you are working now, or one you have worked with recently. Complete the checklist on Line Master 6 (you can get this from your teacher) to analyze whether you are an effective group member.

2. Think of a time when you worked in a group that was successful, and you were proud of what you accomplished. Make a list of all of the things that worked well. Explain what made your group so good.

How to Complete Work in Groups

Before You Start

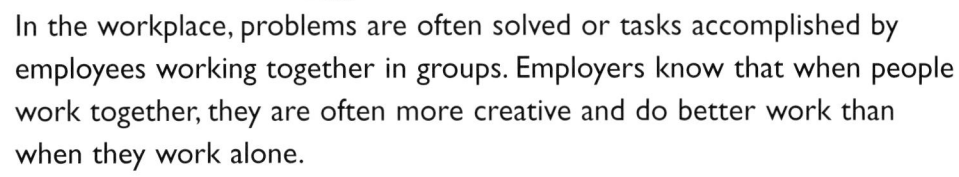

In the workplace, problems are often solved or tasks accomplished by employees working together in groups. Employers know that when people work together, they are often more creative and do better work than when they work alone.

But getting things done in groups can take lots of time, commitment, and patience. People in groups need to learn and practise strategies that will help them achieve their tasks effectively.

Before you follow these steps to completing a research task in a group, think about these questions:
- What do you like about working in a group?
- What do you find challenging about working in a group?

Do It Yourself

Step 1 Gather as a group and visualize what the final product might look like. Decide what needs to be done to get there. Take turns giving your ideas. Then ask yourselves:

Who is our reader? What will that person want to know?
What graphics will we need?
What information will we include in our writing?
Which points have come up more than once?
Which ideas do we all like? What's missing?
What length will the final product be?
How much time do we need to do the work?

Step 2 Set group goals. Turn your ideas into categories or subtopics that will give a focus for your research. Draw a picture or create an outline of what your final product will look like, and give each group member a copy. Create a timeline or plan for accomplishing your task. Decide what the group is going to achieve each day.

- **Step 3** Decide who is going to research which subtopic and discuss some research strategies. Discuss where you might find the information you need, and who can help you (see How to Research, pages 54-57). Use the outline you've created to record your information. Renegotiate your timeline if necessary.

- **Step 4** Work independently to complete your research. Look at your deadline and work backward to figure out when you will need to do your research. Bring your outline when you do your research. Write your points on the outline.

- **Step 5** Share your research with your group in any way you choose. (You might each pass your research to one another and comment directly on the work, or you may share your information orally.) When all of the information has been shared, ask questions about the total research: Do we have enough information? Do we have the right information? Do we need to do more research?

- **Step 6** Discuss in your group the best order for your subtopics. Create a new outline of your product. This time, cut and paste (by hand or by computer) the subtopics and the details in order. Read your new draft aloud to the group, and reach an agreement on the order.

- **Step 7** Decide as a group how to format the information. What do you want your reader to know and remember? What will help the reader locate the information quickly and easily? If you were the reader, what would help you?

  Create a draft of your own subtopic information in the chosen format. Share your new drafts by passing them around and commenting on them. At this point, make notes on clarity, completeness, and irrelevant detail. (Edit for spelling, grammar, and punctuation later.)

  Make the suggested changes to your draft.

- **Step 8** Edit your revised draft to achieve correct spelling, grammar, and punctuation. Give your edited draft to another group member for proofing. Continue the editing process until your draft is perfect. Recopy your draft, incorporating the changes.

- **Step 9** Arrange the edited subtopics on blank paper in the agreed order. Together decide which design features (italics, bold, underline) will help the reader understand the main points. Make the changes.

- **Step 10** Before choosing the visuals and graphics, reread the edited print drafts in order. Ask yourselves:
  Would key visuals, photographs, or graphics help the reader to understand each section better?
  What might these look like?
  What do we have room for?

  Together arrive at a decision. Then decide who in the group is going to create or find the graphics that are needed.

- **Step 11** Create your layout, experimenting with a number of ways of arranging blocks of print and visuals on the page. Vote on each arrangement. Which design is the most pleasing to look at? Which design makes the print easiest to read?

- **Step 12** Together decide on a way to create the final copy (a computer-created product; a manual cut-and-paste) and how all group members can help.

Hot tips

- During brainstorming, listen to everyone's ideas. Don't say yes or no — list as many ideas as possible.
- Select one person from the group to record ideas.
- If two people want to work on the same subtopic, they can choose straws (one long, one short) or draw a card from a hat ("first choice," "second choice,").
- While ordering your ideas, think again about who your reader will be. What is the first thing s/he will want to know? What's the next thing?
- While editing, read your work aloud to hear unfinished sentences.
- Highlight words that don't look right or grammar that you are not sure of.
- Use classroom resources and your personal dictionary and spelling list to help you correct your errors.

Making It Work: Language

This model describes some work that a group is going to do. What elements do you think will be the responsibility of all group members?

Model

group members — Vlad, Demetri, Shairose, and Ashley are working together to <u>create</u>
task — a one-page fact sheet for Career Day. The fact sheet is about a
length of fact sheet — career which interests all of them. They must do the following: — time limit

steps in group task:
- research this career
- take notes, organize, draft, revise, and edit the information
- decide on accompanying visuals and graphics, and produce an effective layout that balances print and visuals
- produce the final copy

Think about It

How could the group members divide the work they need to do? Suggest a plan for the group.

Use the Anthology

Using "Sunshine Getaways" (pages 235–236) and "The Beautiful Bruce Peninsula" (pages 222–227) as samples, and following the steps for a group research project, create a travel brochure or guide to a vacation destination of your choice.

Activity

1. Work in a group of four people to design and produce a fact sheet on a career of interest to all of you. Present your completed fact sheet to the class.

2. Analyze how well your group worked as a team to complete its task. What worked well? What would you do differently next time?

How to Create a Personal Dictionary

Before You Start

We all have a personal vocabulary, or a bank of words, that we use to communicate. You can make your personal vocabulary bigger by keeping track of interesting and useful words that you read or hear in films, television, books, conversations, and more. A personal dictionary will help you gather the words that are important to you in school and in the future.

Before you follow these steps to creating a personal dictionary, think about these questions:
- How would keeping a personal dictionary help you?
- How can expanding your vocabulary help you as you enter the workplace?

Do It Yourself

Step 1 Decide where to keep your personal dictionary, and how to organize it. Consider using:

A section of your writer's notebook: Create a tabbed section in your notebook, starting with one looseleaf page (front and back) for each letter of the alphabet. Enter each new word on the appropriate page.

An insert in your writer's portfolio: Create your own booklet, bound or stapled, leaving two or three pages for each letter of the alphabet.

A section of your reading response journal: Create a space on each page of your response journal for useful or interesting words. It could be a box on each page or a column (like a margin).

A small spiral notebook: Keep the notebook in a pocket or schoolbag. Create a section for each letter of the alphabet.

Index cards: Record words on index cards. Keep them in a box, arranged alphabetically.

Making It Work: Language

- **Step 2** Decide what your typical dictionary entry will look like. Use a format (see the models below) that highlights the word and its meanings. You can also use graphics and visuals.
- **Step 3** For each dictionary entry, include:
  - the word, spelled correctly, written in a way that stands out
  - the meaning(s) of the word, either from context (what it means in the reading passage) or from the dictionary
  - words that can be built from the same word, or that share the same root (see Line Master 7, available from your teacher).
  - synonyms for the word (words that mean the same thing), which you can find in a dictionary or thesaurus
- **Step 4** Add to your personal dictionary. List words that interest you while you are reading, listening, or viewing, then complete the entry for each word.
- **Step 5** When you write, look in your personal dictionary to check spelling or to find an effective word. If you find a compelling word in another source while you're writing, add it to your personal dictionary.

HOT tips
- Write down interesting or new words that you encounter when reading, watching movies or television, or during a discussion. Later you can add them to your personal dictionary, along with their meanings.

Here are some formats for setting up a personal dictionary. Which one do you think would be most useful for you?

Model 1

Chart

shows word, meaning, related words, and synonyms in a chart

Word	Meaning	Word-building	Synonyms
technician	An expert in a technique or master of technical skills	technology, technical, technique, high-tech, technological	skilled worker, expert

Model 2

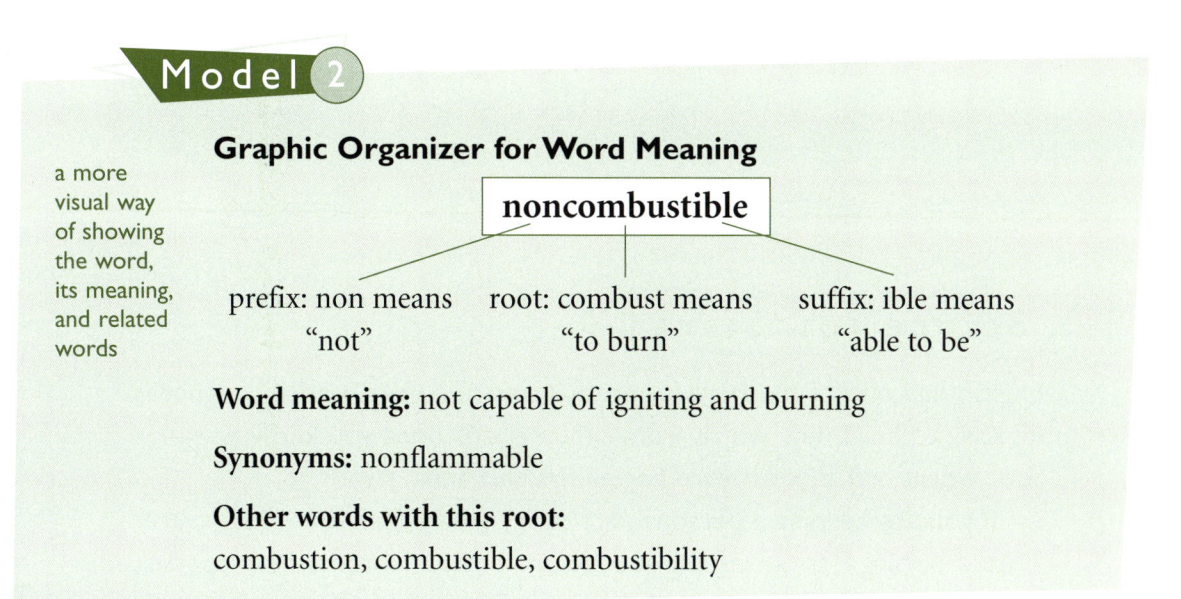

a more visual way of showing the word, its meaning, and related words

Graphic Organizer for Word Meaning

noncombustible

- prefix: non means "not"
- root: combust means "to burn"
- suffix: ible means "able to be"

Word meaning: not capable of igniting and burning

Synonyms: nonflammable

Other words with this root:
combustion, combustible, combustibility

Think about It

Why is it useful to know the meanings of some key word roots, prefixes, and suffixes? Why is it useful to create your own dictionary? (See Line Master 7 and Line Master 8, available from your teacher.)

Use the Anthology

From your reading of informational and business forms in the anthology, choose ten useful words to add to your personal dictionary.

Activities

1. From an article you have just read or are about to read on the topic of a potential career, choose five or more words that are specific to that field. Use one of the suggested models for recording the words in your personal dictionary.

How to Build a Specialized Vocabulary

Before You Start

English has one of the largest vocabularies of all the world's languages. It's easy to build new words from other words once you know common root words and affixes (word beginnings and endings).

If you are keeping a personal dictionary (see pages 121–123), you're already keeping lists of words that build upon common roots. Most specialized vocabulary in English is built on Latin and Greek roots. Once you recognize the meanings of these root words, you can apply what you know to your reading and writing.

Words can be divided into two parts:

The **root word** (or base word) is the part of the word that contains the basic meaning.

The **affix** is the part of the word that is added before or after the root word to add to its meaning. A prefix is added to the beginning of the root word. A suffix is added to the end of the root word.

Before you follow these steps to building specialized vocabulary, think about these questions:

- What do you usually do when you read a word that you don't understand?
- What kinds of things do you read that have a specialized vocabulary?
- Give two examples of words that are made up of smaller words.

Do It Yourself

Understanding Specialized Vocabulary

- **Step 1** Choose a word to examine. It might be a scientific or technical term, a specialized word from a workplace that interests you, or a word that your teacher assigns.
- **Step 2** Write the word in your notebook. Identify the root word and underline it.
- **Step 3** Find and write the meaning of the root word.

Steps

● **Step 4** Look at the affix or affixes to the word. Use what you know about the meanings of the affixes (see Line Master 8, available from your teacher) to figure out the meaning of the word.

For example, exobiologist = exo + bio + log + ist — person
   | | |
outside life an area
              of learning

exobiologist — one trained to study life on other planets

Do It Yourself

Creating Specialized Vocabulary

● **Step 1** Use what you know about how words are made to create a new one. Think of something you would like to describe, such as a job that you do or a place that you work.

● **Step 2** Find a root word that has the base meaning for that word. Look at your personal dictionary for root words, or get Line Master 7 from your teacher. Write the root word in your notebook.

● **Step 3** Add the affixes that give your word just the right meaning. You will find a list of affixes on Line Master 8, available from your teacher.

Hot tips

- A new word is called a "neologism" (from neo = new + logos = word).
- Advertisers use new words to name new products. Entrepreneurs use them to name new companies. They use parts of words that customers already know, and combine these to create a name that will make sense (Compubuy Advisors Inc. is a company that gives advice to customers about which computers to buy).

Here is an example of an invented word that describes a certain idea.

Model

idea: an expert about computer fears
root words: compu, phobia
affixes: log, ist
new word: compuphobologist

Think about It

As our knowledge of the world expands, we need more and more new names for things. What groups other than advertisers and entrepreneurs make up new words and names for things?

Use the Anthology

In the excerpt of "Boom, Bust & Echo 2000" (pages 37-41), find five specialized words. Divide each word into parts, and use what you know about root word meanings, suffixes, and prefixes to build the meaning of the word.

Activities

1. Add to your personal dictionary by finding the meanings of the following words. Identify the root of each one. Choose three of the words. Use their roots and the affixes on Line Master 8 (available from your teacher) to create a new word for each root.

    prejudice

    solution

    emigrate

    export

    territory

    instruct

    geometry

2. Choose a scientific or specialized term from one of your school subjects. Find the root. Create three related words by adding prefixes and/or suffixes.

3. Using some common root words, add prefixes and suffixes to make up your own term for each of:

   a 21st-century career

   a product for the marketplace

How to Create a Personal Style Guide

Before You Start

Almost every writer finds some aspect of grammar, spelling, or punctuation difficult. Good writers know their own writing problems and work hard to correct them.

By creating your own guide to the conventions of the English language — your personal style guide — you'll have a resource that is designed especially for you and that will help correct the grammar, spelling, and punctuation errors you make most often.

Before you follow these steps to creating a writer's guide, think about these questions:
- What are your strengths in writing?
- What mistakes do you make most often in your writing?

Do It Yourself

Steps

● **Step 1** Decide where to store and how to organize your style guide. You might like to do one of the following:

- Create a tabbed section with looseleaf pages in your English binder or writer's notebook. You might want a section for each of spelling, grammar, and punctuation so that you can find your references easily.
- Create a bound or stapled booklet with enough pages to write grammar, spelling, and punctuation rules and reminders. Keep the insert in your writer's portfolio.
- Divide a small spiral notebook into sections for your grammar, spelling, and punctuation rules and reminders. Keep it in a pocket or schoolbag.

How to Create a Personal Style Guide

- **Step 2** Brainstorm a list of the things you need to improve in grammar, spelling, and punctuation. Using information from your teacher or your own insights, think about what words, phrases, types of sentences, and punctuation you are usually unsure about. (The checklist on Line Master 9, available from your teacher, can help you to record your observations.)

- **Step 3** For each item you need to improve, write a rule or a reminder in the appropriate section of your style guide. You can find this information in published style guides, grammar books, and dictionaries, or from class lessons. Record only the rules that you need to improve your own writing.

   Write your rules and reminders in your own words so they are helpful to you.

- **Step 4** Use your style guide. Once you are ready to edit a piece of writing, examine it closely for accuracy of the language. Highlight, circle, or underline anything which doesn't sound right, or that you are unsure about. Then consult your style guide to check your grammar, spelling, or punctuation rule or reminder.

   Continue adding to your style guide. While editing, you might find that you need a rule or reminder that you haven't recorded. Find the rule and add it to your style guide.

Hot tips

- Revise your ideas before you edit for grammar, spelling, and punctuation. Ask yourself: Have I said everything I want to say? Will my reader understand my piece? Are there any irrelevant details? Is everything in the right order?

Here is a sample of how one writer notes her questions when she edits her first draft of a letter she has written to the school newspaper. Why are Sandy's questions to herself helpful?

Model

(should this be a comma, or is this correct?) — **Dear Editor :**

We the older students need to do more to make sure that our new grade nine students feel safe and welcome at our school.

sp? —

Just two days ago I (past) a little grade nine girl just outside the gym lockers. She was crying. At first I was (embarased) and walked by.

— sp?

can I start a sentence with but? — But then I went back and asked her what was wrong. She didn't want to talk about it but she was so upset that she finally told me. Ever since school started an older girl was taking her lunch money. Now the girl wants more. She didn't want to go to the office to report it, but she was also really scared and didn't know what to do. That's why she was crying. It seemed to me that the best thing I could do was to be like a big sister and (walked around) with her between classes so the other girl would get the message and stop picking on her. (Its) working!

— verb tense?

or it's? —

I think that if every grade nine kid had an older friend to trust and talk to, then every grade nine like my new friend would make a better adjustment to high school life. Anyone interested in helping (run-on sentence?) — me start a program for this please contact me in 11C homeroom.

(capital?) — Yours (T)ruly,
Sandy T.

Think about It

Choose one grammar problem, one spelling problem, and one punctuation problem that Sandy has identified in her letter. For each one, write a rule or reminder that Sandy could record in her personal style guide.

Use the Anthology

Read "My Fair Lady" on pages 53-60. Consider how Eliza Doolittle uses grammar. Create a short style guide that would help her improve her grammar.

Activities

1. Examine your strengths and weaknesses in grammar, spelling, and punctuation. Choose a piece of writing that you've done recently and reread it. What grammar, spelling, and punctuation in this piece are you unsure about? Highlight, underline, or circle words, phrases, and punctuation whose correctness you wonder about.

2. Using one or two writing pieces that your teacher has marked, make notes on the checklist on Line Master 9 (available from your teacher) about the things you do well and the things you need to improve about your spelling, grammar, and punctuation. For those items which you have marked "I need to improve," write a rule or reminder in your style guide.

How to Choose Appropriate Language

Before You Start

Every writer writes with a real audience in mind. The writer wants the target audience to understand what he or she is writing, and chooses a style that will hold the interest and match the skills of those readers. The writer chooses words, phrases, and the kinds of sentences that the reader will recognize and understand. The writer also uses the form of writing that will reach the audience best — for example, a letter, an essay, a report, or a story.

When you write, remind yourself who will be reading your writing, and choose sentences and words that will keep the attention of your readers. If you are writing something for your peers, you will use a different style from one you would use if you were writing the same piece for young children.

Before you follow these steps to choosing appropriate language, think about these questions:

- Why is it important that we choose words and types of sentences that are right for our readers?
- What might happen to a reader's understanding if the writing style isn't appropriate?

Do It Yourself

Step 1 Before writing, ask yourself the following:

Who is my audience?
What might the audience know about the topic?
What do I want the audience to know about the topic?
What might the audience want to know?
Why do I want the audience to know about my topic?
What form of writing will help me to interest this audience?

How to Choose Appropriate Language

Steps

- **Step 2** Choose a point of view.
  - First-person point of view: Use "I" as the main voice to make the writing more personal.
  - Third-person point of view: Use "he/she/it" as the main voice to make the writing more objective.

- **Step 3** Choose a form of verb.
  - Active voice — "Juanita slammed the door with a crash, leaving Benito frustrated and betrayed." — Active voice gives a sense of immediate action and purpose. Active voice makes the reader feel close to the subject or part of the action.
  - Passive voice — "It soon became known that the emperor was dead, and his name was spoken with awe and reverence." — Use the passive voice if you don't know who is doing the action, or if you want to create a sense of objectivity or distance.
  - Imperative verbs — "Take the next turn, and you will come to the edge of the world." — Use the imperative to give instructions or commands, or to draw the reader into the text.

- **Step 4** Choose the type and complexity of words and sentences you want to use.
  - Common words and shorter sentences are easily understood by a broad or young audience.
  - Specialized and technical word, phrases, and sentences are suitable for more specific audiences.

Hot tips

- Note your audience and purpose at the top of your piece of writing to remind yourself of what writing style to use.

Here is a piece of writing done for a newsletter. What words and phrases in the first paragraph create the writer's tone?

Model

Getting Your Boat Ready for Launch

by the First Mate of *Intrepid*

As all you fishers, sailors, and charter boat operators know, March is the best time to start thinking about getting your boat ready. Now, I know that the boats don't get launched here in Ontario until late April or May, but it never hurts to get started early.

The first thing you need to do is to determine if you need to add another coat of anti-fouling paint on the hull. Walk around the boat a few times at high noon and see if you can spot any bare spots. Although you have to apply most anti-fouling paints within 48 hours of launch, it's always good to know what you have to do.

The second thing to determine is that all of your underwater fittings are well-sealed and that none of them will leak. The last thing you want is to get your boat in the water and to start seeing it fill with water. You may need to take off the through-hull fittings and reseal them in new caulking just to make them watertight. Last year at our boatyard, someone left a valve open, and the boat sank in no time flat. His boating season was off to a terrible start.

Another thing you need to do is to check that your impeller for your knot-meter moves easily. One summer I had to haul my boat out of the water to replace it mid-season, and I vowed to put it on my checklist before launch every spring.

A final important pre-launch item is to flush your inboard engine of the antifreeze you took in last fall. Antifreeze in our lakes and rivers is extremely toxic to fish and other wildlife, so always leave enough time before launch to flush your engine. Be sure to catch the antifreeze in a container and dispose of it responsibly.

Well, that's my checklist for a smooth launch. I wish you all fair winds and a safe season of boating.

Annotations:
- author knows audience
- first person
- active voice and imperative verbs bring the reader in
- some technical words for a special audience
- slang words make the tone friendly
- complex sentence for older audience

Think about It

Who is the intended audience for this piece of writing? What does the audience know about the topic already? What does the author think they should know?

Use the Anthology

Read "Confessions of a Freak" (pages 32-33). What words and phrases does the author use that tell us that she is a teenager writing to a teenage audience?

Activities

1. Plan a piece of writing which will give students in your local elementary school some information about a particular program, activity, or event in your high school. Ask yourself the questions in Step 1 (page 132), make predictions about your audience, and record the decisions you make about your writing style.

2. Think about an event that has taken place recently in your school. Write a letter describing the event to two very different audiences:
   - a friend who goes to another school
   - an adult or parent

   Think about the differences between the two letters. Consider and compare:
   - the choice of words
   - the sentence complexity
   - the tone of voice

How to Make a Presentation

Before You Start

The challenge when you make a presentation is that your audience only has one chance to take in your information. A presentation works well if it:
- captures the audience's attention right away
- clearly tells the audience the purpose of the presentation
- is just the right length to keep the audience's attention
- informs the audience about what they need to know
- satisfies what the audience might want to know
- uses language that is right for the audience's understanding
- has ideas that are clear and well thought-out
- is organized logically

Before you follow the steps to preparing and making a presentation, think about these questions:
- What makes an oral presentation interesting to you? What things keep you listening until the end?
- What do you find enjoyable about doing oral presentations? What do you find challenging?

Do It Yourself

Steps

- **Step 1** Choose a topic, or use one that you have been assigned.
- **Step 2** Think about what you know about your topic. Brainstorm a list or use a visual or graphic organizer.
- **Step 3** Think about your audience. Ask yourself the following questions and note the answers.

   What do I know about the audience?
   What do I need to tell my audience about the topic?
   What do they know about this topic already?
   What will interest them about this topic?

> What might they like to know about this topic?
> How long will I be able to keep them interested?
> What will I need to say to keep their attention?

- **Step 4** If necessary, gather additional ideas for the presentation.
- **Step 5** Organize your presentation ideas into an outline. You can use Line Master 5 (available from your teacher), or a word processing or presentation program, to help you create your outline.

    First, make a statement about the topic of your presentation and your purpose. Next, make a few statements about what you think the audience already knows about the topic. Keep this section short so that your audience doesn't lose interest.

    As soon as you can, pose a question, or make a statement about an interesting fact that the audience probably doesn't know, or make a controversial statement that not everyone will agree with (this will increase attention and interest.)

    If you've asked a question, you can give the answer followed by your facts, details, and supporting evidence, or give the facts and evidence and let them lead you to the answer later in the presentation.

    If you've given the audience an interesting or controversial fact or thesis to consider, give the evidence, facts, and details that explain it, support it, or prove that it's true.

    End the presentation by either re-asking the question you began with or restating the controversial or interesting fact. Close with a summary statement that generally answers the question or supports the statement.

HOT tips

- Plan and organize the content of your presentation based on what you know about your audience. Keep your audience's attention by keeping your points short and by using interesting information and visuals.
- Fit the number of facts and details, and the amount of evidence to the amount of time that you have to do the presentation.

Here are a writer's notes and final presentation. In what ways do you think the fact sheet was helpful to the writer?

Model 1

topic

Topic of Presentation: The Sinking of *Titanic*

Notes:

information gathered about the sinking of the Titanic

- the ship was believed to be "unsinkable" because it had separate bulkheads that could be closed if they were ruptured, sealing off the water from the rest of the ship
- it was one of the largest ocean liners ever built
- it had two sister ships: the *Olympic* and the *Britannic*
- the captain (Capt. Smith) was trying to set a record for the fastest ocean crossing
- it was on its maiden (first) voyage when it sank
- it sank early in the morning of April 15, 1912
- it was intended to be the captain's last voyage — he was supposed to retire immediately after the voyage
- the ship sailed from Southampton, England and was supposed to dock in New York
- the ship carried 2224 passengers, but because it was believed to be unsinkable, it had lifeboats for only 1178 people.
- it was a luxury ship, but many of its passengers were not in first- or second-class. They were travelling in the lower parts of the ship, called the "steerage" section.
- the ship was warned that it would be passing through an iceberg field, but it didn't slow down
- 1513 people died; only 711 were rescued

beginning of presentation

Presentation

statement that will be backed up with facts during presentation

Today I'm going to explain the real reason why *Titanic* sank. Many people think the reason was just bad timing and bad luck. But what really caused the sinking of *Titanic* was human pride.

Titanic was one of the largest ocean liners ever built. She had two sister ships, the *Olympic* and the *Britannic*. *Titanic's* first voyage was from Southampton in England to New York City in April of 1912. She was carrying 2224 passengers.

The builders believed that the ship was unsinkable. If it hit anything that punctured the hull, that bulkhead would be sealed off to prevent water from entering the rest of the ship. For this reason, *Titanic* only carried about half the life rafts it needed for the passengers on board. — facts that back up initial statement

The owners of *Titanic* wanted to set a speed record on her first ocean crossing. As the ship approached the east coast of North America in the early morning hours of April 15, the crew was warned that there were icebergs ahead, but they didn't slow down. *Titanic* hit an iceberg, which tore a huge hole in its hull below the waterline. There were too many bulkheads to seal off. The ship sank in just over an hour. There was a ship nearby, but it didn't hear *Titanic's* distress call.

Only 711 people were rescued. 1513 people died. Many of these had been travelling in the lower part of the ship, the steerage section. The Captain, who'd intended to retire when he reached New York, went down with the ship.

If the builders hadn't been so proud of their unsinkable ship, they'd have made room for enough life rafts for all of the passengers. If the owners hadn't been so proud, the ship would have slowed down through the iceberg field, and the tragedy wouldn't have happened. Therefore, it was human pride that caused the sinking of the *Titanic*. — restatement of points / conclusion

Think about It

At what point does the speaker introduce the purpose of the presentation? Why is this an important thing to do? What facts and details support the speaker's point? How does the speaker make sure that the audience remembers the main point?

Use the Anthology

Choose one of the five unit themes of the anthology. Choose several selections from that unit and write a presentation that explains how the selections support the theme.

Activities

1. Read the facts about the sinking of *Titanic* in the model. Imagine that you had to turn these facts into a presentation for your English class. Create a profile of your class as an audience. Use the notes and your profile to create an outline for the presentation you would give.

2. Imagine you are a salesperson. Choose a product or service that you represent and on which you have to give a presentation to a potential customer. Make notes on the product information, then create an audience profile of the customer. Write an outline of the presentation you would deliver, and deliver the presentation to your class.

How to Conduct an Interview

Before You Start

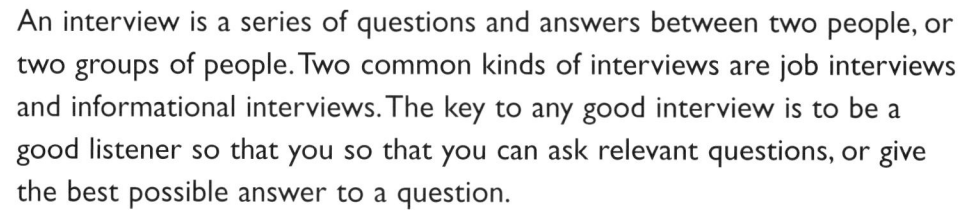

An interview is a series of questions and answers between two people, or two groups of people. Two common kinds of interviews are job interviews and informational interviews. The key to any good interview is to be a good listener so that you so that you can ask relevant questions, or give the best possible answer to a question.

Before you follow the steps to conduct an interview, think about these questions:

- What do you do now when you prepare for an interview?
- What questions do you expect to be asked in an interview?

Do It Yourself

Step 1 Know the basics of your interview — the topic, the interviewee, and the purpose.

Step 2 Arrange a time and place for the interview. Both should be convenient for the interviewee.

Step 3 Research the topic or person briefly. Ask yourself: What do I already know about the person or topic? Why am I interested? Why did I choose this person or topic?

Step 4 Write at least five questions that cannot be answered with a yes or no — questions that really interest you about this person or topic. Think about and write questions that ask who, what, where, when, why, and how (the 5 Ws and H). When you've written your questions, ask yourself: Will the answers tell me what I want to know? Will the answers tell others what they want to know? If not, then change your questions.

Once you've created the questions, decide on the order in which you should present them. It's often best to start with easier, more routine questions and leave the more sensitive questions to the end.

Leave wide spaces on your paper to record answers, or write each question on a separate sheet of paper or an index card.

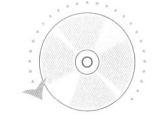

Making It Work: Language

- **Step 5** Gather all of the materials you need, from pen and paper to batteries and a video camera, and make sure you know how to use them.
- **Step 6** Arrive at the interview ahead of time to set up your equipment.
- **Step 7** Begin by introducing yourself to the interviewee. Remind him or her of your purpose in conducting the interview. Start your interview with a question about the interviewee's interests. This will help make him or her more comfortable and more open to answering difficult questions. As you ask your questions, take notes. If necessary, ask the interviewee to pause to give you time to write down the responses. Next, move on to the routine questions. Finally, ask any sensitive questions.
- **Step 8** Thank the interviewee for his or her time. Later, send a thank-you note and, possibly, a copy of your final product.
- **Step 9** Use the information gathered to write your report, summary, or article. If you use an exact quote, use quotation marks. If you agree with the interviewee that something is "off the record," do not include it in your final product.

Hot tips

- Newsletters, annual reports, a company's Web site, newspaper articles, and trade publications are good sources for research before your interview.
- Make sure you have a neat appearance.
- Shake hands firmly and show that you are confident because you are well prepared.
- Check the spelling of the interviewee's name.
- Speak clearly, make eye contact when you can, and avoid chewing gum and using slang.
- Be interested, enthusiastic, and a good listener and recorder.
- Audiotape or videotape the interview, with the interviewee's permission, so that you can record quotes accurately.
- Check your notes and recordings after the interview. Contact the interviewee if something is unclear or to verify quotes.

How to Conduct an Interview

These are models of the questions asked at an informational interview and a job interview. What is different about the questions asked at each interview? What is similar?

Model 1

Informational Interview

open-ended questions:
- How much education and work experience are needed for your job?
- What are some of the challenges you have faced in your job?
- What is a typical day like for you?
- What are some of your job achievements?
- If you changed jobs, what future direction(s) would you like to take?

Model 2

Job Interview

- Is there anything you would like to know about our company? — *to learn what research the interviewee has done*
- Why would you like to work for our organization?
- What skills and strengths could you bring to this position?
- What do you find challenging or difficult about your current work?
- Why did you leave your last job? — *to encourage interviewee to understand positive side of all work experiences*
- Tell me about a time when you demonstrated responsibility. — *to encourage interviewee to describe behaviour*
- Tell me about a time when you recognized a problem and corrected it.
- Tell me about a time when you showed leadership.
- Give me an example of a group situation when you used strategies for conflict resolution. What were the results?

Think about It

What is the purpose of each of these types of interviews? Think of one question to add to each interview.

Use the Anthology

"Lost ... and Found" (on pages 34-36) is also an interview. Are the questions in that interview more like the ones in the job interview example or the informational interview example? Why do you think that is so?

Activities

1. Interview a friend or mentor in the workforce about his or her career. What kind of interview will this be?

   First, write your five key questions. You might ask about such topics as achievements, choices, challenges, future directions, duties, associates, and expectations.

   When you have completed the interview, write a summary, beginning with an introduction to get your readers interested. Next, choose the material from the interview that you think is the most important and interesting. Finally, write a concluding sentence. Have someone edit your work.

2. Read interviews in magazines and newspapers to see how they are done. Imagine that a friend is going to be interviewed by a reporter for a magazine or newspaper. What advice would you give him or her before the interview?

Media

TABLE OF CONTENTS

Media around You	146
How to Search on the Internet	150
How to Identify Elements of, and Create, a Magazine or Newspaper	154
How to Analyze and Create a Radio News Report	160
How to View a Television Program	165
How to Identify Bias	170
How to Analyze and Create Advertising	174
How to Create a Storyboard	180
How to Create a Video	184

Media around You

What exactly are media? They are the different things that entertain and inform us: movies, songs, computers, television, radio, magazines, newspapers and more. What is your favourite of each one?

In your notebook, list the media that entertained you this week. Then list the media that supplied you with information this week.

▸ Analyzing media

This section of the handbook will give you lots of strategies to help you analyze media. In general, when you examine a media product, you need to consider who is saying what to whom, with what purpose, and what result.

What influences media creators?

This word web shows you the elements that media creators keep in mind. Creators choose their format based on how much money it will take to create it and what kind of technology they have available. They think about their own editorial policies (the kind of information they'll agree to include in their product) and about standards in their industry (such as standards for what information can be included in an ad). They also think about their purpose for creating that product and the message they want to share.

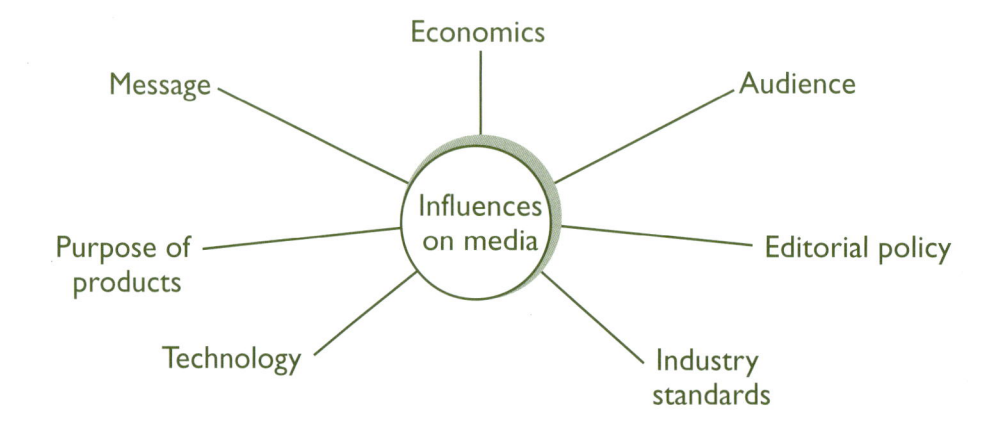

Influences on media:
- Message
- Economics
- Audience
- Editorial policy
- Industry standards
- Technology
- Purpose of products

What kinds of media formats are there?

There are many formats for media. Each format was once separate from the others, but now the formats have all started to merge. Newspapers have become aligned with television stations, radio stations have created Web sites, the Internet uses video, and advertisements are found everywhere.

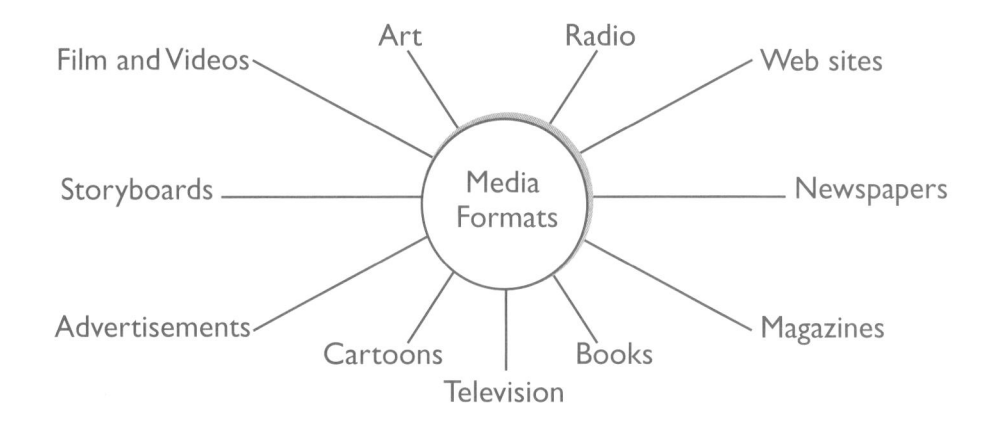

Media Formats:
- Film and Videos
- Art
- Radio
- Web sites
- Storyboards
- Newspapers
- Advertisements
- Magazines
- Cartoons
- Books
- Television

Who is the audience?

The audience for a media product can be any of these:

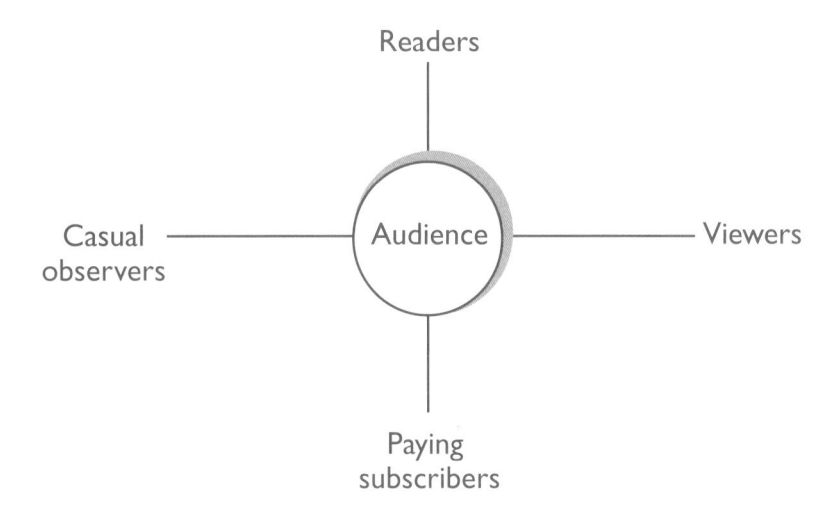

Audience:
- Readers
- Viewers
- Paying subscribers
- Casual observers

Making It Work: Media

▶ Make the connection

When you view media of any kind, connect the form and production options, the purpose, and the audience. This practice helps to make you an active, critical viewer of media so that you understand how media works are designed to influence audiences and reflect the perspectives of their creators.

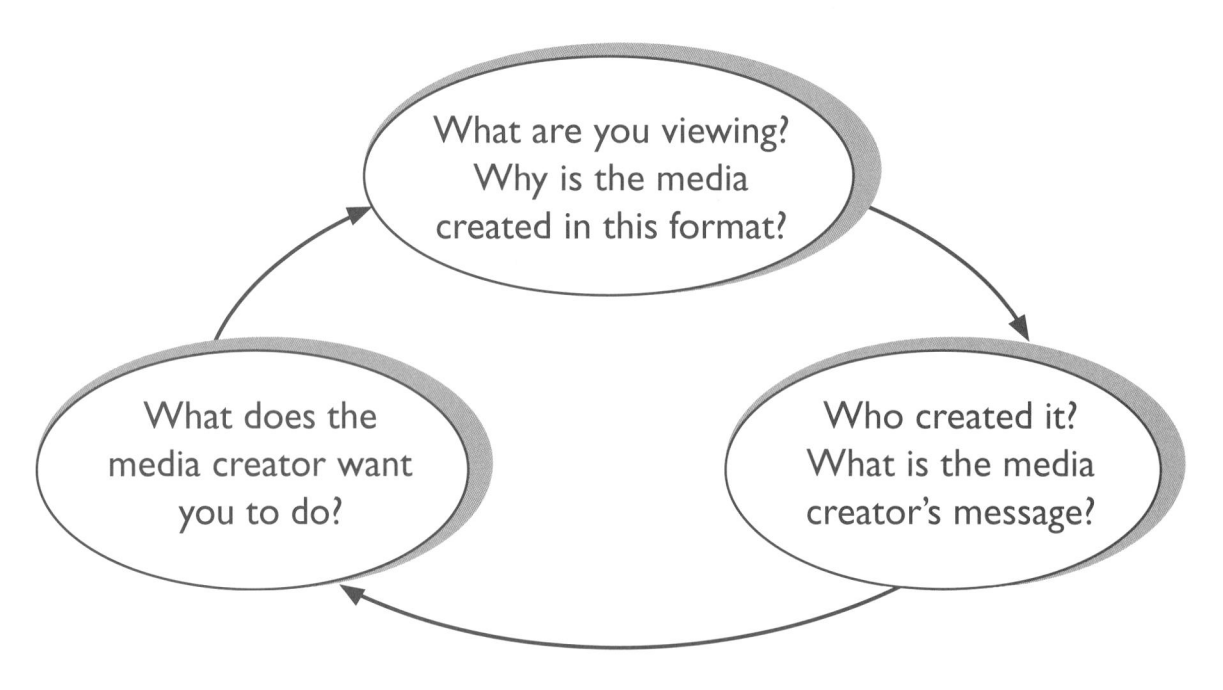

- What are you viewing? Why is the media created in this format?
- Who created it? What is the media creator's message?
- What does the media creator want you to do?

Media in the workplace

Observing media

Media are a tool for communication. They are used in the workplace to instruct and inform. You may see training, safety, procedural, and informational videos at work. You need to be able to view actively, take the information, and apply it to your job. You can use the tip below when you watch any visual media.

- Take notes while you watch. Note the main idea and the details that support it. Think about cause and effect relationships. Think about how you can apply the information.

Creating media

Most workplaces use advertising. As an employee, you may be asked to create a sign or an ad. You can use the tip below when you create any kind of media.

- Think about the message, the audience, and the format you are going to use (colour, shape, size, design, line, pattern, framing).

Think about it

In your notebook, record answers to the following:
- What aspects of media would you like to explore?
- What media skills would you like to improve?
- What media skills will you need for the careers you are considering?

Keep your responses in mind as you read this chapter so you can pursue areas that will interest and help you.

How to Search on the Internet

Before You Start

The Internet is the name for a group of worldwide information resources or sites hooked together by computers. Through the Internet, you can do many things, from research to reading a newspaper to doing your banking to buying groceries.

ABird the Internet is a good place to begin research for reports or job searches. But there are challenges involved with using the Internet. The information you find there may not be accurate. If a site is not maintained, the information on it may be outdated. Always support your Internet research with other sources.

Before you follow these steps for searching on the Internet, think about the following questions:
- What Internet searches have you done? Were they successful? Why?
- How can you determine if something you have found on the Internet is accurate?
- What sites do you prefer to use for research? Why?
- What do you think are the pros and cons of Internet access in the workplace?

Do It Yourself

Steps

Step 1 Before you can begin a search on the Internet, you will need access to a computer and a modem, as well as an Internet service provider. Use a computer at home, school, the library, or, with permission or for work-related issues, your workplace.

Step 2 Use your valid user ID and password, known as your login, to begin your session on the Internet. To visit a specific site on the World Wide Web, you need to know its address, called a URL (Uniform Resource Locator). Type in the URL at the top of your screen after "Go To" or "Location". Most URLs begin with http://www.

Step 3 If you are looking for general information or don't have the URL you need, use a directory search, such as www.yahoo.ca. Choose the directory that best matches the subject you are researching (for example, travel, news, history).

How to Search on the Internet

The directory searches the Web for you and displays what it finds. Sometimes the sites are useful to you — sometimes they are not.

Step 4 If you have a specific topic, use a search engine, such as Lycos, Netscape, or Altavista, available at your Internet home page. Type your topic in the blank space shown for searching. Use as few words as possible in order to get as much information as possible. If you want to do a more specific or "advanced" search, follow the search engine's steps.

The search engine will search the Web and provide you with a list of sites. Many search engines will list a percentage to tell you how closely the site matches your topic.

Step 5 When you find a site that interests you, click on it to go there. You can either begin to use it for research right away or add it to your list of bookmarks or favourites. If you bookmark the site, you can go back to the search engine and check other sites. When you are ready, you can use the bookmark to return to the sites that you have saved.

Step 6 When you include researched information in your writing, you need to list, or cite, where you found that information. For information you gather from a Web site, include the name of the Web site and the address of the page where you found your information, and, if possible, the author and the date of posting. (For more on citing sources, see How to Research, step 4, page 55.)

Hot tips

- Any person can create a Web site. Be cautious about using online information — not everything you read is true or accurate.
- For the best chance to get reliable, updated information, choose the Web sites of large or very stable groups, such as government agencies, large organizations, universities, and newspapers.
- Use the links you find on various Web sites. Links take you to other Web sites that may have the kind of information you are looking for.
- Web sites include a lot of information. Read slowly and carefully to make sure you find what you need.

Making It Work: Media

> **Hot tips**
>
> - Good resources for projects are:
>   - The Internet Public Library (http://www.ipl.org)
>   - Rogers: Electric Library Canada (http://www.elibrary.ca)
>   - Encyclopedia Britannica (http://www.encyclopediabritannica.com)
> - Good resources for job searches are:
>   - HotJobs (http://www.hotjobs.ca)
>   - Human Resources Development Canada, National Youth Site (http://youth.hrdc-drhc.gc.ca)
>   - Youth Resource Network of Canada (http://www.youth.gc.ca)

This is the home page of www.monster.ca, a job-search site. What are the first three things you notice when you look at this Web page?

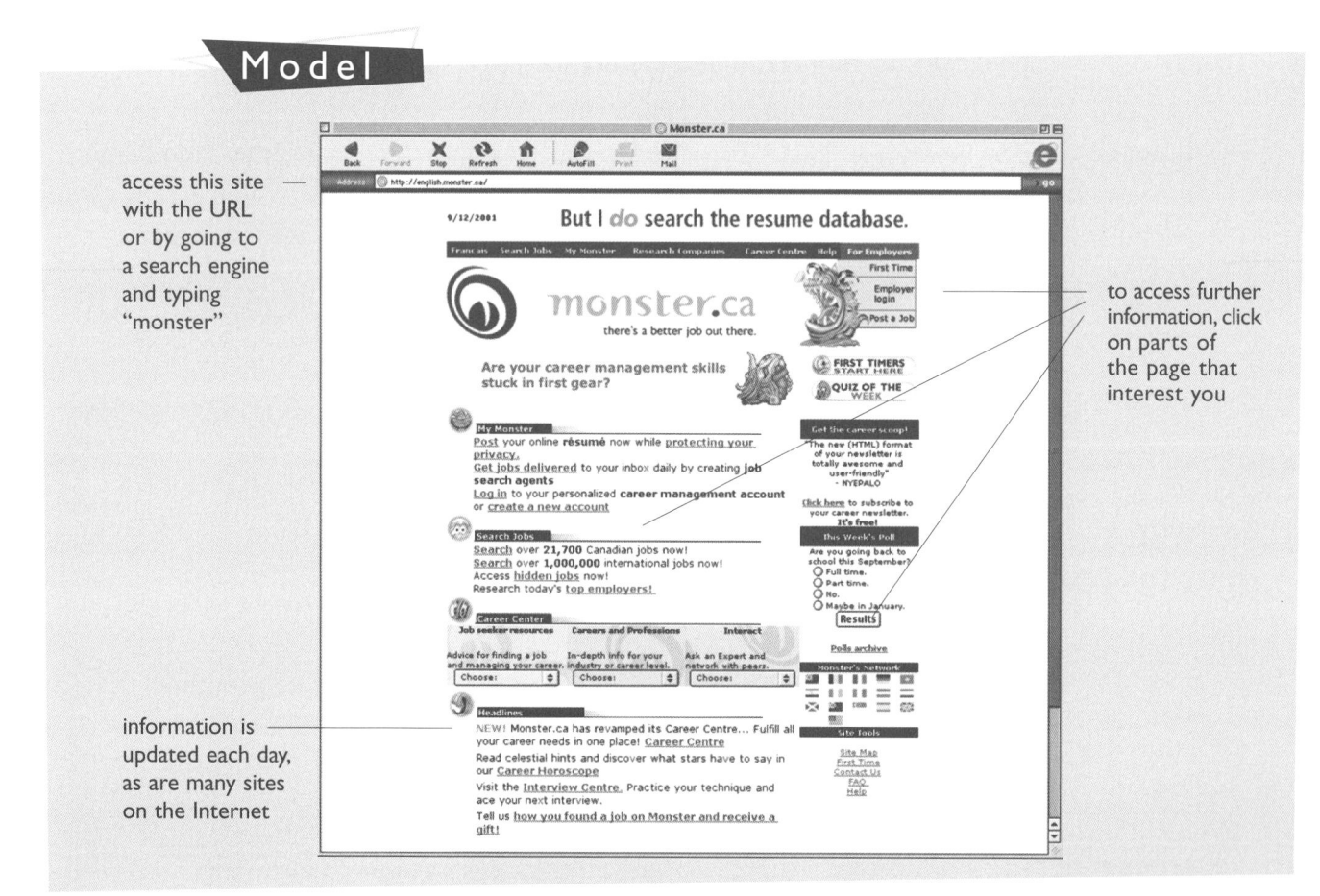

Model

- access this site with the URL or by going to a search engine and typing "monster"
- to access further information, click on parts of the page that interest you
- information is updated each day, as are many sites on the Internet

Think about It

Look at the home page of yahoo.ca, a search directory, on page 56 of the Handbook. What are the similarities and differences between yahoo.ca and monster.ca?

Use the Anthology

You will find the home page of the Canadian Youth Business Foundation on pages 208-209 of the anthology. What makes it look different from the home page of monster.ca?

Activities

1. Complete an Internet search on a topic assigned by the teacher of this course or for something you are studying in another course. Use a computer at school, work, home, or the library. Remember to cite your sources accurately (see How to Research, pages 54–57).

2. As you do your Internet search, evaluate the Web sites you visit. See if you can find any examples of bias or inaccurate information (see How to Identify Bias, pages 170–173). Here are some questions to consider in your evaluation:

   What are the qualifications of the authors?
   Do the authors include their opinions?
   Is there a fee to get the information?
   Who is the intended audience (students, children, scholars)?
   Who created the Web site (government, individuals, an organization)?
   When was the site created?
   How often is it updated?

   Evaluate at least three sites that you visited. How do they compare?

How to Identify Elements of, and Create, a Magazine and Newspaper

Before You Start

Publications are created with a reader in mind. Publishers think about what the reader wants to read, how the reader wants the publication to look and be organized, and what message they want to get to the reader.

Before you follow the steps to analyze a publication, or create one of your own, think about:

- How are magazines and newspapers different? Similar?
- Why is it important to think carefully about what you read in a publication?

Do It Yourself

Identifying the Elements of Magazines and Newspapers

Steps

Step 1 Read the contents page of the publication to find out what kinds of elements the publication includes. Take notes of what you find. The publication might include some or all of the following:

— News stories: They may cover local, national, and international issues. News stories answer the 5 Ws and H — who, what, where, when, why, and how. They begin with a lead (introduction) and move from the most important points to the least important points. In a magazine, a news story or an article might begin with a deck. The deck is a lead printed in a larger type than the body text. Its purpose is to get the reader's attention.

— Articles: These are stories, profiles, and information about a variety of topics such as sports, entertainment, fashion, food, lifestyles, and so on.

— Editorials: Editorials contain opinions, and can be humorous, controversial, moving, and/or informative. They are written by an editor or editorial team. They are like essays and have an introduction, a body, and a conclusion.

- Display advertisements: They are ads with a dominant visual element, such as a slogan or picture. Newspapers sell space for these ads to help cover the cost of producing the paper.
- Features: These are in-depth, human interest articles.
- Columns: The parts of the publication in which writers express their opinions on, and their analysis of, various issues.
- Letters to the editor: This section provides a forum for readers to contribute their comments about issues covered.
- Cuts: These are items such as photographs, comics, art, graphs, and maps, which illustrate the articles.

Step 2 Look through the publication to see how the type and pictures are placed on the page. This placement is called the layout. Layout techniques break up the type and organize the issues. Make notes about the layout techniques you notice. This might include considering: columns; headlines (titles); sub-heads (titles within the article); fonts, type styles, and sizes; colour; page numbers; consistent page design; balance of white space; cutlines (captions under cuts/photos); jumplines (continuations of the articles to other pages); and groupings of types of articles into special sections.

Step 3 Read several selections in the publication. You will notice that the writing is correct and clear, and includes quotations, a logical development of thoughts and ideas, conciseness, and originality.

Step 4 Make note of the differences between a magazine and newspaper. Differences might include size, paper quality, news coverage, and the type and placement of advertisements. Because of the size and colour of the magazine and the quality of its paper, it lasts longer than a newspaper. But because magazines are published less often than newspapers, they can miss reporting on big events or report them some time after they have happened.

Making It Work: Media

Do It Yourself

Creating a Magazine or Newspaper

Steps

- **Step 1** Decide on a theme or issue for your publication. Identify your target audience.

- **Step 2** If you are working in a group, assign duties for the issue. For example, you will need one or more editor, reporter, and designer. Together, decide which sections your publication will include, and what will go in them. Consider including editorials, and articles covering entertainment, sports, news, and features. The editor or editors should assign the articles and make sure there is a good balance of reporting. If you are working alone, you will perform all of the duties.

- **Step 3** Research your articles and write them in the proper format. The selections The Writing Process (pages 50–53), How to Research (pages 54–57), How to Write a Paragraph (pages 58–61), and How to Write an Opinion Paper (pages 62–66) will be helpful.

    Articles begin with leads that summarize facts, ask questions, or otherwise grab a reader's attention. The lead should offer the most important information about the story. Articles are broken into short paragraphs. For news articles, begin with the most important details, then give the important details, and end with the least important details. News articles do not need to have conclusions. Each story should be accurate, original, and relevant. Include research sources and quotations where necessary.

- **Step 4** As a group, meet to comment on one another's work. If you are working alone, ask someone you trust to read and comment on your work. Edit and revise your work.

- **Step 5** Choose a font and type size for the publication. Type articles and set them in columns. Create art, advertisements, cartoons, photographs, or graphs to accompany the articles, as well as any other visuals you need. Keep in mind that you should have a dominant photograph or other type of cut (art) on each page.

- **Step 6** Create a dummy, or a rough layout, of your publication by folding together sheets of paper (one sheet of paper folded in half creates four pages of a magazine). Using pencil, sketch out what will go on each page.

    Make sure you have included all the elements you want, and that everything is placed where you want it.

How to Identify Elements of, and Create, a Magazine or Newspaper | **157**

> ● **Step 7** Lay out your publication with a good balance of type and white space. Avoid clutter. Lay out the cuts (art) first, then the cutlines (captions), articles, and headlines. A cut goes first because that should be the dominant element on the page; it is what the reader looks at first. Use a jumpline if you need to continue a story on another page. (Try not to over-use jumplines; they bother readers.) Include an index to organize the issue.

Here is the front page of the Thunder Bay *Chronicle-Journal*. What is the first thing you notice about this page?

Model

- **masthead** – the nameplate of the newspaper; includes name, city, and date
- **top story** – at the top of the page, it gives what the newspaper considers the most important news of the day
- **cut** – a visual feature, such as a photograph, drawing, chart, map, or graph
- **cutline** – the line of type under the cut that provides information about it
- **index** – lists main sections and page numbers; helps readers to find what they want to read
- **newspaper's Internet address**
- **headline** – title of the article
- **lead** – the first one or two paragraphs of an article
- **body** – the details of the article that follow the lead
- **byline** – the name of the writer of the article
- **jumpline** – directs readers to where the story is continued

Making It Work: Media

> **HOT tips**
> - Smaller newspapers subscribe to a wire service, such as the Canadian Press (CP), to gain access to world news stories via satellite. You may see wire service names or initials after the dateline on a news story.
> - When you read, think about how accurate the stories in the publication may be. Don't believe everything you read.

Think about It

Which elements on the front page of the Thunder Bay *Chronicle Journal* are organizational tools? Which elements are designed to get people to buy the newspaper?

Use the Anthology

You can find other examples of items from newspapers and magazines on pages 30–31, 115–116, and 228–231 of the anthology. What elements of the sample on page 157 of this handbook do you see on those pages? What elements are not there? Why do you think that is? What makes the magazines look different from the newspapers?

Activities

1. Evaluate the coverage of local news in your area, either in print or online. If there is a daily paper where you live, focus on its coverage of your community's news for one week. If there is a weekly paper where you live, focus on its coverage of your community's news for one month.

    Cut out all local news stories, editorials, editorial cartoons, and opinion pieces. Date each item and underline the lead. Organize your clippings by such categories as crime, health and safety, sports, education, law, labour, the arts, and government. Then glue them into a scrapbook by category, in order of date.

    Create a bar graph to show the number of stories that appeared for each category. Answer the following questions in complete sentences. Write them in your scrapbook or glue in a printed copy from the computer.

a. Did page one emphasize local news more than provincial, national, or international news during the week of your analysis? Why or why not?

b. Describe any bias shown in the clippings (see How to Identify Bias, page 170)?

c. Were local events and issues also the subject of pictures, editorials, editorial cartoons, letters to the editor, or other opinion pieces? Refer to examples.

d. Which local story did you like the best? Why?

e. Summarize in two paragraphs your evaluation of the newspaper's coverage of local news.

2. Choose a magazine to analyze. Write three paragraphs exploring the overall content of the magazine. Consider these questions in your analysis:

   a. What devices do the photographers, layout artists, and writers use to get the reader's attention and make their point. (Consider, for example, colour, cuts, typeface, and arrangement of content.)

   b. Describe the content of the magazine.

   c. What do the readers hope to gain from the magazine?

   d. What do the creators of the magazine assume about their readers' interests, attention spans, levels of education, class, age, and gender? How can you tell?

   e. How is your attention attracted to the articles? (Note the use of headlines, pictures, and the layout itself.)

   f. How does the layout (or page design) of the magazine make reading easier for the reader?

   g. What are the general strengths and weaknesses of the magazine?

   h. Do you think the magazine will remain successful? Why?

3. In groups, create a newspaper or magazine covering a theme or issue related to this English course. For instance, you could create a specialty issue about everything you need to know to succeed in the workplace.

How to Analyze and Create a Radio News Report

Before You Start

We get our news from television, radio, the newspaper, and the Internet. Each has its own way of delivering information, and we have different reasons for using each one as a source of news.

Before you follow the steps for analyzing and creating a radio news report, think about these questions:
- What source do you use to get your news?
- When do you listen to the radio and why?
- What qualities of radio make it a good way to get news?

Do It Yourself

Analyzing a Radio News Report

- **Step 1** Listen to several different radio news reports. Most stations have a newscast every hour on the hour. Listen to the news on at least three different stations.
- **Step 2** Create a three-column chart to compare the newscasts. Label the columns with the station name and the length of the newscast.
- **Step 3** Answer the following questions to help you analyze the newscasts in general. Record your answers for each station on your chart.

> What kinds of news stories are reported? What is the order of the stories?
> Is an editorial part of the newscast? When is it offered?
> How many news readers are there?
> How would you describe each news reader's tone of voice?
> Is the news straightforward or sensationalized?
> How much time is given to each story?

- **Step 4** Select a story that is covered in all three newscasts. Answer the following questions for each station's coverage.

  > Did the story include an interview?
  > Were any sources cited for the story?
  > What was the introduction, or lead, to the story? Was it effective?
  > What are the answers to who, what, where, when, why, and how in the story?
  > How much detail was included in the story? How does that compare to the amount of detail in a newspaper story?

- **Step 5** Write an analysis of the three different newscasts you heard. How are they the same? How are they different? Which one is most effective? Least effective? Why?

- **Step 6** Use the answers to Step 4 to write an analysis of how different stations treat the same story. Why do you think they are similar? Different?

Hot tips

- Try to review the radio news reports more than once.
- Prime time on the radio is 7:00 a.m to 9:00 a.m. and 4:00 p.m to 6:00 p.m. These are the hours when many people are travelling to and from work or school.
- Most people keep the radio on for short periods of time, so it's important to give information quickly but completely.

Do It Yourself

Creating a Radio News Report

Steps

- **Step 1** Choose a topic for your radio news report.
- **Step 2** Research the topic, using the newspaper, the Internet, and television news reports as sources.
- **Step 3** Decide whether your report needs just your reporting from the studio, or if it also needs an eyewitness or someone reporting from the scene.
- **Step 4** Write the script for your news report. Begin with one or two sentences that answer the 5 Ws and H. Add the details that describe and explain your first sentence. Add any other details you think are important. Add information from an on-the-scene witness or reporter, if you need it.
- **Step 5** Revise your report. Make sure your introduction, or lead, is interesting. Does it get your listener's attention? Does it provide all the information you need to share? Complete a good copy of your report.
- **Step 6** Practice saying your report aloud. Time your spoken report. Is it short enough to keep your audience's attention, but long enough to give all the information? Deliver your report to a small group, your teacher, or the whole class.

Hot tips

- Listen to radio news to hear how newscasters speak, what words they emphasize, and how and when they change the tone of their voice.

How to Analyze and Create a Radio News Report | 163

Here are two examples of news reports that you might hear on the radio. What information do you get from reading (or hearing) the first sentence of each one?

Model 1

what, when, where, who, why, how — "The area's first fire of the New Year began early this morning at a home in the old Main Street area. Fire officials estimate the fire began around 12:30 a.m. A passerby noticed smoke and immediately called the fire department. It is believed that the fire originated in the basement of the home. The owner, Joe Smith, was absent at the time. Luckily, no one was injured. Live on the scene is Tania Hassan. Tania, can you tell us the cause of the blaze?" — voice of news anchor (news reader in studio)

"Richard, the cause of the blaze has yet to be determined. The Fire Marshall is investigating the remains of the 25-year-old home for clues. Firefighters suspect that faulty wiring may have been the cause. Damage is estimated at $300,000. I have Mr. Smith with me now in front of the smoky remains of his home. Mr. Smith, what are your reactions to this terrible fire?" — voice of field reporter (reporter at the scene)

"I'm just grateful the New Year's Eve party wasn't at my house this year! Thank God no one was injured and the firefighters had it under control quickly." — witness's voice

conclusion — "Richard, fire officials remind everyone to have a working smoke alarm. Live on Main Street, I'm Tania Hassan for

radio station's call letters — XYZ News." — reporter's name and location repeated

Model 2

announcer identification — "I'm Sue Delmonico at the sports desk. To the hardwood — GM Glen Grunwald today announced that the Toronto Raptors have signed fan favourite Jerome "The Junkyard Dog" Williams to a huge seven-year deal worth $42 million. With Antonio Davis already signed, Grunwald can sink a three-pointer by signing Alvin Williams when he meets with the player's representatives tomorrow morning. If he wants to keep superstar Vince Carter happy — and you can bet that he does — Grunwald needs this group of players for another chance to sink that final basket and bring an NBA championship to Toronto."

- who
- what
- when and where
- how
- why

Think about It

You usually have ony one chance to hear a radio news broadcast. What devices help make these two reports interesting and easy to follow?

Use the Anthology

Choose a newspaper article from the anthology. What information might not be included in a radio news report about the same story?

Activities

1. Create a radio news report by following the steps shown on page 162. Your report should be for the 6:00 p.m. newscast on a station that gives a straightforward newscast. Research, write, revise, practise, and tape your report. Label your tape and submit it.

2. Listen to a number of stations with different formats. Each station has a target audience it tries to draw and keep. How is the news treated on a station whose audience is teenagers? How is the news treated on a station whose audience is the parents of teens? How are the two kinds of newscasts different? What other audiences might a radio station target? How might that change the way it treats its news?

How to View a Television Program

Before You Start

If you watch television, take the time to be an active viewer, giving full attention to what you watch. Look for the messages being shared, whether in a music video, an ad, the news, or a documentary, and try to understand how television affects you.

Before you analyze a television program, think about these questions:
- Do you watch television?
- If you do watch television, do you take time to reflect on what you watch? Why?
- What do you like to watch on television?

Do It Yourself

- **Step 1** Choose a television program to watch.
- **Step 2** Use a list of questions, like the list shown here, to help you focus on what you are watching.

> 1. Why do I feel the way I do while I watch?
> 2. What is the theme of the program?
> 3. How do the effects (music, lighting, sound) influence my response?
> 4. How is the content influenced by:
>   - the audience the show wants to attract? (gender, age, social class)
>   - the format of the show? (half-hour, hour)
>   - the purpose of the show? (information, advertising, entertainment)
>   - the editorial policy of the show? (certain acceptable themes, messages, language, values)
> 5. What techniques are used to appeal to teenagers? How would older and younger viewers react to these techniques?

6. Is what I'm watching real or true? Are the characters believable? Do the props and costumes add to the believability? Are any of the images electronically altered?
7. Does the program use sensationalism?
8. How do elements such as plot, characters, dialogue, narration, setting, and body language contribute to the program?
9. Do I like or dislike this program? Why?
10. Why is the program popular or unpopular?

Step 3 Watch the program and take notes based on the questions in Step 2. Include examples to illustrate your points.

Step 4 If possible, view the program a second time. Add any comments you wish.

Hot tips
- Consider keeping a viewer journal, where you respond to what you have seen. A viewer journal is also helpful if you are analyzing a program for class, and need to count shots or critique elements such as acting, effects, or dialogue.
- Notice how the mood is set by dialogue, body language, colours, lighting, and music.

This page is taken from a script of the **CBC** television show *Foolish Hearts*. In this excerpt, a director is telling film students about the importance of the camera. What elements (such as music or lighting) are described that you think will affect a viewer watching this television program?

Model

       1 TITLE SEQUENCE: YELLOW SCRIPT OVER RED   1
          SATIN FIELD

music —   MUSIC: "FOOLISH HEART" (INSTRUMENTAL SECTION)

          FADE TO BLACK.

2 INT. STUDIO   2

    PETER, the DIRECTOR, SPEAKS as we <u>HEAR activity on</u>   —— sound
<u>the set</u> over black.

        DIRECTOR <u>(V.O.)</u>   ——voice-over
        More than any other element in the
        making of a film, I love the lights.
        The lights seduce me.

ANGLE ON A HUGE HMI. It explodes on high, <u>silhouetting the</u>   ——lighting
<u>Director and INTERVIEWER</u> with microphone - a STUDENT
FILM CREW (use film school students). High in flies on rig.
It descends during . . .

        DIRECTOR
        I often have to struggle against the
        impulse to turn the camera away from
        the scene and shoot them.
        I doubt that they teach that in your
        film school.

<u>ANGLE ON more LIGHTS</u> as they turn on.   ——lighting

        DIRECTOR
        (continuing)
        Without light, there's no contrast
        and without contrast,
        there's no art.

<u>ANGLE DOWN ON</u> the FIRST A.D.   —— camera angle

        FIRST A.D.
        Let's have the camera! And get the
        band ready to rehearse.

        DIRECTOR
        Next comes the camera. The camera's
        function is to place a frame around
        the action, and of course, record it.

Some push in an <u>apartment corridor flat,</u> set it up, and light it.   —— setting

> DIRECTOR
> (continuing)
> I can hear your film professor saying, that's absurd, a film starts with the script, with the word. But, for me, the script pages are no more than a convoy of trucks that carry instructions from the director's imagination to the workers who put the film together. Though these trucks are essential, they have a tendency to break down, make too much noise, and pollute the atmosphere.
>
> ANGLE ACROSS FLOOR, a woman, 33, in <u>heels and a Chanel suit, hurries in, agitated,</u> followed by a FEMALE A.D. and a MAKE-UP ARTIST. It's HOLLY VANSTONE, the wife.
>
> HOLLY
> <u>I can't believe this is happening! This is like some horrible dream!</u>
>
> ANGLE across vast studio floor. The CAMERA CREW slowly dollies the CAMERA forward out of the BLACK SHADOWS. BAND in street clothes on studio floor warming up. The rig lands. The Director and his interview crew step off the rig onto the floor.
>
> DIRECTOR
> Then come the actors, who, for me, exist only as the characters. I don't know them in their lives off camera.

costumes — ANGLE ACROSS FLOOR...
stage direction — hurries in, agitated,
dialogue — I can't believe this is happening!

Think about It

What does the director in the television script think is the most important element of filming? Why? Do you agree that the script and actors are secondary? Explain.

Use the Anthology

Look at the excerpt from the play *My Fair Lady* (pages 53–60). How are the stage directions for a play different from those of a television program?

Activities

1. In groups, discuss the effects (pro and con) of watching television. The following are some suggestions to get you started:

   Pro:
   - Watching violence on television provides a release so we will not feel the need to hurt others.
   - Television stimulates or encourages people to read.
   - Television increases our vocabulary and improves our literacy.
   - Positive social behaviour is modelled on television.
   - People can learn from educational television programs.

   Con:
   - We watch so much television that we have become a nation of "vidiots."
   - Television has a negative affect on alcohol use, sleeping and eating habits, physical fitness, and stress. Viewers expect problems in their lives to be resolved in half an hour as they are on television; when they are not quickly resolved, viewers become depressed.
   - There is a relationship between viewing televised violence and aggressive behaviour; watching violence on television may cause aggressive behaviour.
   - Television changes our view of appropriate lifestyles and promotes stereotypes.

2. In groups, create a plan for a situation comedy about teenagers in a workplace. Think of situations for the comedy. Decide on characters and their traits. How will your characters be different from or similar to real teens? Write a one-paragraph description of the concept. In a second paragraph, explain why you think the program will succeed and the techniques you will use to help it succeed. In a third paragraph, describe how you could promote or advertise the program. Revise your work before completing your final draft.

Making It Work: Media

How to Identify Bias

Before You Start

A bias is an opinion or preference. The word bias often sounds negative, but everyone has a bias of some kind, shaped by his or her world. Bias can keep us from making objective judgements.

People who make media use things like lighting, sound, and camera angles to give us their message, from their point of view. The choices they make can reflect messages about what to expect of people based on money, looks, age, cultural background, social class, and gender. As a viewer, you need to make your own decisions about the product, values, and beliefs being shared.

Before you follow the steps to analyze media products for bias, think about these questions:
- Have you ever been pleased with, or angered by, a message you noticed in a commercial or television program? Why?
- How could knowing about bias in the media help you in the workplace?
- How do you think the information we get on the news would be affected if the government controlled our newscasts?

Do It Yourself

Step 1 Read the following to help understand different kinds of bias.

Types of bias:
Bias by omission: defining a group without including all information about it
Bias by commission: drawing attention to particular qualities to define or separate a group or person
Implicit (indirectly stated) bias: presenting material from a narrow perspective, or using stereotypes
Explicit (directly stated) bias: presenting a prejudiced view of events, individuals and/or groups

- **Step 2** Choose a media product to view, such as a film, a television program, a newscast, or a documentary. As you watch, take notes to answer the questions below and in Step 3. If possible, view the product more than once.

  If you are watching a newscast, think about the following:
  - What are the top stories? What do you think of the order in which the stories are presented?
  - Does each story qualify as "news" in your opinion? Explain.
  - Are there words and pictures on the screen? How do they change how you understand the news story?
  - Who is reading the news? How does that affect what you think of the news?
  - How do the anchors speak? (Think about their tone and how they deliver the information.)
  - How do the anchors' word choices affect the information they give?
  - Does the anchor give the information in a straightforward way?

- **Step 3** If you are watching something other than a newscast, think about the following:

  Content
  Describe the program. What, if any, is its stated point of view?

  Audience
  Who is the target audience (think about age, gender, social class, education)? How do you know?
  What is appealing about the program to the target audience?
  What is advertised during this program? Are the products and services advertised appropriate for the target audience?
  Is there product placement (the use or appearance of certain brand-name items, such as soft drinks or computers) in the program? What message does that send?

  Portrayal of characters
  How does the program show women, men, children, teenagers, and seniors? Do you think there is bias in how each group is shown? What kind of a bias? Would people from each of those groups think there is bias in how they are shown?
  How does the program show people from various cultural backgrounds? Do you think there is a bias in how they are shown? What kind of a bias?

Making It Work: Media

Does the program show people as stereotypes? (For instance, someone who is poor may be shown as a slob, blondes may be shown as stupid.) If there are any jokes, to whom are they directed? What message do you get from the targetting of the jokes?

Message
What is the theme of the program? What is the main message that you, as a viewer, get from the program?

Step 4 Write a report to share your findings. Follow the steps in How to Write a Report (pages 67–69), or The Writing Process (pages 50–53) to help you.

Hot tips

- Effects such as camera angles, music, sound, body language, and make-up can direct the audience to respond in a certain way (see How to Create a Video (pages 184–187) and Line Master 11 (available from your teacher) for more information).
- When you watch a program, try to question the choices made by the creators of the work.

On the next page are line-ups for a dinner-hour sports news show. One line-up is for the East Coast edition of the show. The other is for the Ontario edition of the show. What do you expect to be different about the stories in each edition? Why?

Model

```
Sports E1              Segment 1
SLUG                   RUNS
HABS/OC                00:26
HABS/VO                00:25

SENS/OC                00:18
SENS/RP                02:07

FLEURY/OC              00:09
FLEURY/VO              00:15
```

```
Sports O1              Segment 1
SLUG                   RUNS
LEAFS/OC               00:19
LEAFS/VO               00:45

ANDERS/OC              00:21

SENS/OC                00:18
SENS/RPT               02:07

FLEURY/OC              00:09
FLEURY/VO              00:15
```

Think about It

Was your prediction about the differences in stories for each edition correct? Why do you think these differences exist?

Use the Anthology

Read the script for "Drop the Beat" (pages 210–218.) Answer the questions in Step 3 in response to that script.

Activities

1. Watch a Canadian program on television. How does it portray Canadians? What are the messages in this portrayal? What bias is shown in this portrayal?

2. Examine the images and the spoken words in a documentary. How do they relate to one another? Report your findings to the class in an oral presentation.

How to Analyze and Create Advertising

Before You Start

An advertisement is a message that helps sell something (such as a product, a service, or an idea) to an audience. Advertisers research to learn about their audience, then find the way they think is best to send their message.

The most common kinds of ads are:

— display ads (print ads with a picture, found on billboards, newspapers, magazines, and the Internet)

— classified ads (usually found in newspapers, paid for by the word or line, organized by type or class)

— commercials (ads you see on TV or hear on the radio)

Before you follow the steps to analyze, and then create, an ad, think about the following questions:

- What recent ads have caught your attention? Why?
- What ads do you dislike? Why?
- What ads do you really like? Why? What message do you get from it?
- Why is it important to think carefully about an ad's message?

Do It Yourself

Analyzing Advertisements

Step 1 As you look at an ad, ask yourself some or all of the questions that follow. See Line Master 12 (available from your teacher) for a description of design terms. See the ad on page 177 for an example of these terms.

1. A display ad
   - How does the ad attract the reader's attention? (Consider colour, headline, body copy, font, images, and so on.)
   - How does the ad interest the reader in the product? (How is the product displayed? How are techniques such as humour used? How is a mood created?)
   - How does the ad create a desire for the product? (Consider the claims made and the logo.)
   - How does the ad urge the reader to act? (Consider phrases such as "limited time offer", "on sale", and "two for one".)

2. A commercial
   - What product is being advertised?
   - What different things happen in the commercial?
   - What visual images stand out?
3. Does either kind of ad use any of the following appeals? This product...
   - has been around for a long time and will continue to be reliable
   - is something everyone uses
   - is used by a well-known person
   - will make you look like you have class and money
   - will make you look attractive and sexy
   - will show you are a person who keeps up with the times
   - is inexpensive
   - will help you find love
   - will keep you healthy and/or safe
   - will save you time
4. A display ad
   - What type of display ad is it? (An *image ad* sells an image of the company, a *sale ad* promotes a price reduction to clear merchandise, and a *promotional ad* refers to special events like school formals, or special times like Canada Day.)
   - How does the body copy (the words under the picture) help you understand the picture?
   - How does the picture add meaning to the body copy?
5. A commercial
   - Describe the people in the commercial. What qualities do they seem to have? How are these qualities associated with the product?
   - Describe the mood of the commercial. How is this mood created? (Consider lighting, music, colour, and body language.)
   - Is there anything suggested beyond the surface meaning of the commercial? (Look at body language, interactions, and product placement.)
   - How do the camera angles contribute to the overall effectiveness of the commercial (see Media Techniques, page 186)? Count the number of shots and describe the pace of the commercial.

Step 2 Identify the target audience of the advertisement by age, socio-economic background, and/or gender. Give evidence from the ad to explain why you believe this to be the audience.

Making It Work: Media

> **Step 3** Look at how you described the ad in Step 1. Consider the audience you identified in Step 2. Write a few sentences to describe how effective the ad is for the audience.

Do It Yourself

Creating Display Advertisements

Steps

- **Step 1** Consider a career that interests you. What product/service might the job promote, or what product/service might be useful to someone in that career? Create an ad for that product or service.
- **Step 2** Think about the information a buyer would need, and what visual images you want to show the buyer.
- **Step 3** Create a store name or company logo, an attention-getting headline for the ad, and an interesting visual of the product.
- **Step 4** Think about how your ad will capture the reader's eye. Select a dominant element (such as a picture, or a large, colourful, or interesting-looking headline) and the other elements you want to use.
- **Step 5** Keep the layout simple and uncluttered by balancing the space you use with empty space (white space).
- **Step 6** Decide if you need body copy to describe the benefits of your product. Sometimes no body copy is needed. You may want to indicate regular price, sale price, associated products, or amount of time the product is available. Use simple language and include believable claims.

HOT tips

- Advertisers try to appeal to intellect and/or emotions.
- Advertisers try to relate their product to things that people need and want, such as health, looks, love, and security.
- Radio advertisers rely on words only and tend to use poetic devices like imagery, symbolism, alliteration, repetition, and appeals to the senses.
- White space is the empty space left when an ad or article is laid on the page. White space helps to balance an item on a page, and helps focus the reader's eye on the main message.

How to Analyze and Create Advertising | 177

What is the first thing that comes to mind when you look quickly at this display ad?

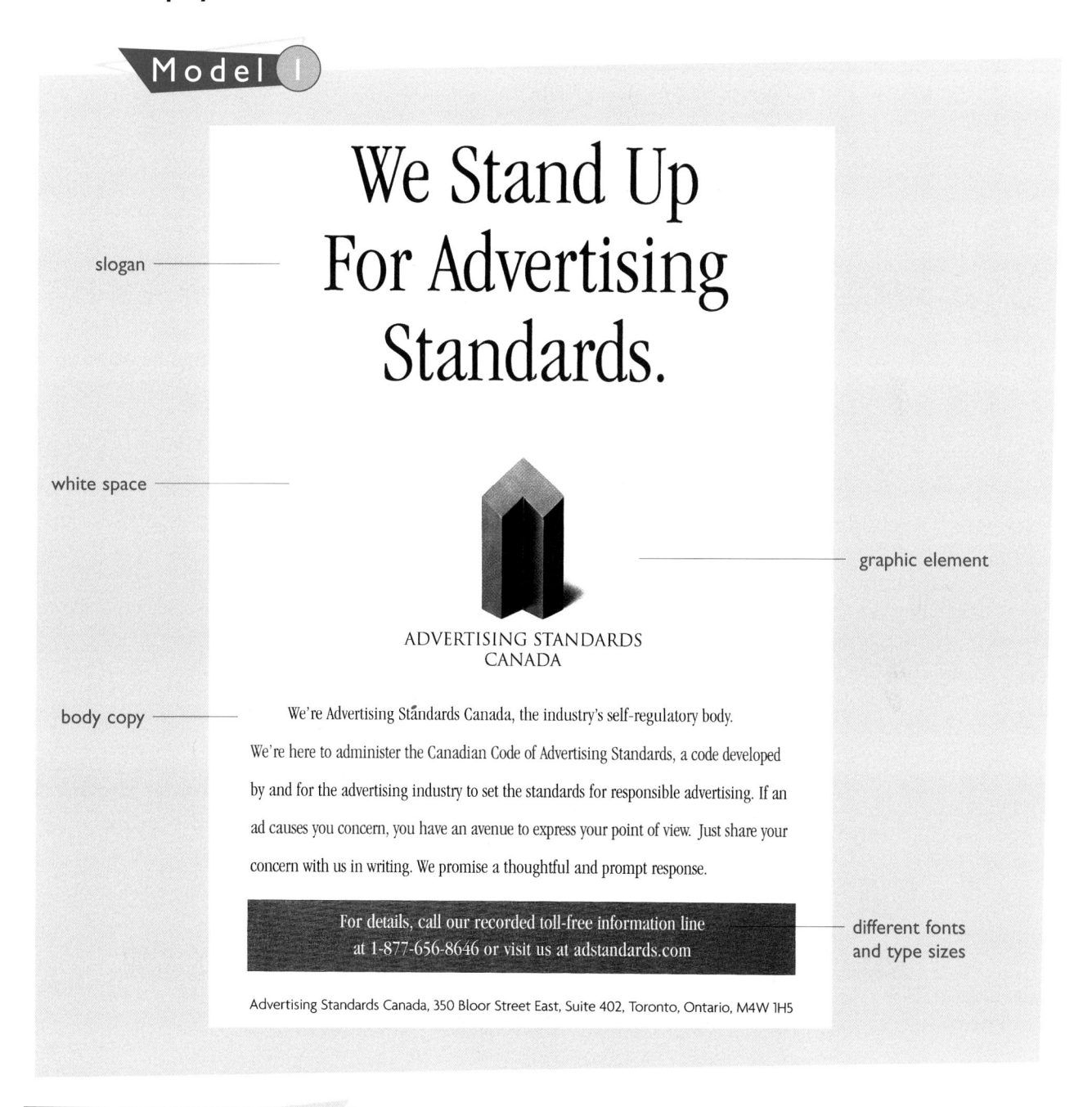

Model 1

slogan —

We Stand Up For Advertising Standards.

white space —

graphic element

ADVERTISING STANDARDS
CANADA

body copy —

We're Advertising Standards Canada, the industry's self-regulatory body. We're here to administer the Canadian Code of Advertising Standards, a code developed by and for the advertising industry to set the standards for responsible advertising. If an ad causes you concern, you have an avenue to express your point of view. Just share your concern with us in writing. We promise a thoughtful and prompt response.

For details, call our recorded toll-free information line at 1-877-656-8646 or visit us at adstandards.com

— different fonts and type sizes

Advertising Standards Canada, 350 Bloor Street East, Suite 402, Toronto, Ontario, M4W 1H5

Think about It

What is your opinion of the slogan for this ad? Is it effective? Why or why not?

Making It Work: Media

Do It Yourself

Creating a Classified Advertisement

Steps

- **Step 1** Decide the purpose that your classified ad would serve. Ask yourself: Do I want to buy or sell something? Am I looking for a job?
- **Step 2** Make point-form notes about the important information you need to include in your ad. Decide on the best order for the information to appear. Write a draft of your ad.
- **Step 3** Check your advertisement, keeping in mind that you pay by the word or the line. Is every word you used necessary? Have you included your phone number or address? Have you included all of the important details, such as price or wage?

Hot tips

- Use short forms or abbreviations of words if you are paying by the line instead of by the word. This will save space.
- Read classified ads for jobs carefully to be sure you have the qualifications listed.

These are classified advertisements. What elements make them different from a display advertisement?

Model 2

number and subtitle of classified section

Help Wanted	For Sale	Announcements
200 Part-time	300 Merchandise	400 Personals
Pizza Delivery. Students needed to deliver pizzas after school, weekends. Must have a driver's licence. Min. wage to start. 4 openings at Pizza Slices. Call 555-1234 for an interview.	Playstation 2. Used three months. Excellent condition. Asking $350.00. Call 555-6789 after 5:00.	Lina Muller, where are you? 2 yrs since PHS grad, we lost touch. Call Shashi, 555-0515.

— title of classified section

— ad with information

Think about It

Why might some writers of classified ads not use abbreviations?

Use the Anthology

Read "Please Recycle: An Ad Series" on pages 232-234. Analyze it using the steps on pages 174-176 of the Handbook.

Activities

1. Imagine you work for an advertising company. Create an advertising campaign for a product of your choice. The campaign should include television and radio commercials and display ads. Present your campaign to the class.

2. With your classmates, discuss how you think advertisers target teenagers. Answer the following questions. Then use your answers to help you write a class profile that describes how the class thinks advertisers view teenagers.
   - What products are marketed to teenagers?
   - Through which kind of media do advertisers try to target teenagers?
   - What elements (such as music, images, and language) are used in ads targetted to teenagers, and how are they used?
   - What values do advertisers promote in ads targetted to teenagers?
   - What issues (such as peer pressure or the need to belong) do advertisers address in their ads?

3. Find out and describe what steps you would take to place a classified ad in your local newspaper.

4. Prepare a storyboard for a televised public service announcement about a workplace safety issue (see How to Create a Storyboard on pages 180-183). You might make it like a rock video, a testimonial, or a narrative.

How to Create a Storyboard

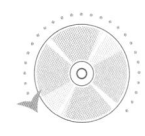

Before You Start

Before directors film a commercial, a video, or even a whole movie, they draw their ideas on a storyboard. A storyboard is a series of frames or boxes, drawn on paper or a computer, that tell a story in order. Each box or frame of the storyboard looks like a view from a camera lens. A storyboard looks like a comic book because it is a series of sketches of the shots, pictures, and words for a script.

Before you follow these steps to create an eight-scene storyboard, think about these questions:

- Have you ever created a storyboard? If you have, what did you like about doing it?
- Why do you think a storyboard is useful in creating media products?
- How do you think a storyboard can help you think through an idea?

Do It Yourself

Steps

- **Step 1** Before you draw your storyboard, you will have to choose your topic and decide what kind of medium you are going to use. Are you creating a storyboard for a commercial, a music video, a documentary, or a short film? Remember to keep your idea simple. Start with an eight-scene storyboard, then move on to longer ones when you have had more practice.

- **Step 2** Identify your target audience. Write a script that appeals to your audience, or write the script as you storyboard. Follow the steps of The Writing Process (pages 50–53) to help you write.

- **Step 3** Make a set of blank storyboard sheets, or divide your paper into eight squares.

- **Step 4** On the first sheet of your storyboard, write your opening idea. In order, write the ideas that follow, one idea per sheet. Each sheet or box will represent about five to ten seconds of film. Number your shots in the order they will be shown in the video.

- **Step 5** Sketch your ideas in pencil first so you can make corrections easily. Do not worry if you are not a great artist; stick figures are fine. When you are happy with what you have created, go over it in marker.

- **Step 6** With each sketch, write a short note about what the character is saying, as well as effects like voice-overs, lighting, camera angles (see page 186), stage directions, and sound effects.

- **Step 7** If you create a film from your storyboard, you can make changes as you work. As you work, feel free to add to, change, or even delete parts of your storyboard.

Hot tips

- You can use a storyboard to share ideas and solve problems, too. With a group, brainstorm ideas about or solutions to a given issue. Use one sheet of paper per topic, and record your ideas on the appropriate page. Order your sheets like a storyboard so that your ideas or your solution flow. Use simple graphics to illustrate each topic.

Making It Work: Media

This is a storyboard of a short film about an issue in the workplace. What information can you get from a storyboard?

Model

Film of "How to Behave at Work"

Scene One

camera angle instructions positioned separately from dialogue and stage directions

Establishing shot; high angle — 1

shot number — Long shot — 2

JOE IS WORKING IN A STORE, STOCKING SHELVES

Joe: Hi Todd, hi Maria.
JOE'S CO-WORKERS COME TO SEE JOE

stage directions in capital letters

Long shot — 3

Close-up of Joe, zoom in — 4

close-up shows a character's head

Maria: Why are you working so hard? The manager's gone today!

Joe: The shelves still have to be stocked. You could help me, guys.

dialogue in boldface

Medium shot of Todd and Joe

Long shot of the 3 workers, low angle

medium shot shows character from the waist up

Todd: Yeah, right! Hey, did you hear what we're going to do this weekend?

Joe: My break's in half an hour. I'll see you then.

V.O.: Joe doesn't let his friends' behaviour influence him.

V.O. indicates voice-over

Think about It

How do the different kinds of shots make you feel about the characters?

Use the Anthology

Look at a play or a screenplay in the anthology. How would a storyboard of the action help you better understand the text?

Activities

1. Choose a scene from a script in the anthology and create a storyboard for it.

2. In groups, storyboard a solution for a work-related problem. For instance, imagine you work in a store, restaurant, or car dealership. People have complained about the customer service. Come up with some solutions to improve customer relations. List everyone's ideas on chart paper and build on them together. See pages 117–120 for group work strategies.

How to Create a Video

Before You Start

Making a simple video is a good way to share ideas visually. In the workplace, employers create videos to sell product, to inform employees, to train employees, and so on.

Before you follow the steps to create a video, think about the following:
- What can you learn from the process of creating a video as opposed to viewing a video?

Do It Yourself

Step 1 Decide what type of media work you will create (for example, a commercial, a music video, a public service announcement, or a training video). If you're not familiar with the format already, watch some examples. Choose a topic for your video.

Step 2 Write a script for your video. Keep your script simple, and think about your purpose and your audience as you write.

Step 3 Think about the tools and techniques used in filming (see Appendix 6, pages 239-240 for more definitions). As you read them, think about techniques that you would like to use in your video, if the equipment is available. Basic elements for making a video interesting are:

> Camera angles: Where you put the camera when you are filming (or the angle of the shot) determines how the viewer sees what you have filmed.
> Lighting: Different kinds of light create different moods.
> Sound: Sound effects can change how people respond to what they view. Voice-overs and narration can add information.
> Music: Music can create different moods or change how people think about something.
> Computer graphics: Special effects with type or art can change the mood of a video.

- **Step 4** Write a storyboard from your script. You can always make changes during filming. On your storyboard, include notes about camera angles, lighting, sound, music, and computer graphics.
- **Step 5** If you are working in a group, you need a director, actor(s), and videographer.
- **Step 6** Practice using the video camera.
- **Step 7** Locate or create sets, props, and costumes appropriate for your script.
- **Step 8** Rehearse the film a few times to be sure everyone knows his or her lines and roles.
- **Step 9** Following your script and storyboard, begin to shoot the film. Make changes to your script and storyboard if you need to. Follow your notes about camera angles and lighting.
- **Step 10** When you are happy with the filming, edit the video using editing equipment or with two VCRs. If you have time and the equipment, add music, sound effects, and computer graphics based on the notes you included with your storyboard.

Hot tips
- Use a tripod to keep the camera steady.
- The more time you spend making necessary revisions to your script and storyboard in advance, the less time you need to spend on location.
- When acting, try to vary your pace, speak clearly, and use appropriate body language.

Using the following techniques can have an effect on your viewer. Which ones do you think you would like to use in a video that you create?

Model

Media Techniques

the camera is positioned below the person or object at a low angle
makes person or object look powerful, important, or strong

the camera is placed slightly below a person's eye level
makes person look aggressive

the camera is positioned above the person or object at a high angle
makes person or object look small, vulnerable, or unimportant, makes toy models look real

object/toy is placed at eye level
makes object/toy appeal to children

camera is positioned at eye level
makes someone look neither really powerful nor really vulnerable

special make-up or costume; shooting through gauze
makes someone look more attractive, younger, slimmer

object is placed one-third down from the top of the screen
draws the eyes to what the director believes is important in the shot

camera tilted; special lighting
adds energy and suspense

Think about It

How can the techniques described on page 186 create hidden messages? What examples of these techniques do you see in commercials?

Use the Anthology

Read "Drop the Beat" (pages 210–218). Find a reference to at least one of the techniques described on page 186, such as a certain camera angle, or a sound effect. What do you think is the purpose of the technique in that part of the script?

Activities

1. Create a safety or training/instructional video for the workplace. Explain your production process when you show it to the class.

2. Find an article in the newspaper about a course theme or issue and make it into a segment for television news. When you are finished, discuss the similarities and differences between the two media forms.

Grammar

TABLE OF CONTENTS

Parts of Speech — 190
- Nouns — 191
- Pronouns — 193
- Verbs — 196
- Adjectives — 197
- Adverbs — 199
- Conjunctions and Prepositions — 201

Sentences — 203
- Sentence Structures — 203
- Common Sentence Errors — 205

Punctuation — 207
- Ending a Sentence — 207
- The Comma — 209
- Other Punctuation — 211

Connecting Words — 216

Direct and Indirect Speech — 219

Using Language — 222
- Synonyms — 222
- Antonyms — 224
- Homonyms — 225

Spelling Rules — 227

Parts of Speech

Before You Start

The different kinds of words that make up sentences, and so make up our language, are called parts of speech. The section that follows identifies many parts of speech, gives examples, and shows how to use parts of speech.

I love to be outside, so I hope that I can get a really interesting job working on a construction site this summer.

- love — verb
- so — conjunction
- that — pronoun
- can get — verb
- really — adverb
- interesting — adjective
- job — noun
- on — preposition
- summer — noun

Nouns

Before You Start

A noun is a word used to name a person, place, or thing. It can also name a feeling, such as fear. There are two kinds of nouns. Common nouns name a thing or group of things without being specific. Proper nouns are names for specific items. Here are some examples.

Common nouns

boy, woman, child, student, choir, home, forest, farm, joy, anger, food

Proper nouns

Nipissing University, Lincoln Alexander, Sioux Lookout, Pelee Island, Montreal Canadiens

MAKING NOUNS PLURAL

When naming more than one of the same item, use a plural.

To form the plural of most nouns:
- add 's' to the end of the noun

  dogs, legs, computers, pianos

To form the plural of a noun that ends in 's,' 'x,' 'z,' 'sh,' or 'ch':
- add 'es' to the end of the noun

  boxes, brushes, churches

To form the plural of a noun that ends in a consonant and then 'y':
- change the 'y' to 'i' and add 'es':

  parties, diaries

To form the plural of a noun that ends in a vowel and then 'y':
- just add 's'

  toys, keys

To form the plural of a noun that ends in 'f':
- change the 'f' to 'v' and add 'es'

  shelves, thieves

Special plurals

- add 'es' to the end of *tomato, potato, hero, echo*: *tomatoes, potatoes, heroes, echoes*
- *roofs, chiefs*
- nouns that keep the same word for singular and plural: *deer, salmon*
- nouns with unique plurals: *women, teeth, children*

POSSESSIVE NOUNS

Nouns can show possession or ownership. Nouns that do this are called possessive nouns.

To form a possessive for a singular noun:
- add 's

Tyrone's hockey stick, the dog's nose

To form a possessive for a plural noun that ends in 's':
- add only an apostrophe

cats' dishes, girls' bikes

To form a possessive for a plural noun that doesn't end in 's':
- add 's

children's hats, geese's wings

Act on It

Read "Rising Threats of Violence in Schools Concern Police" (Anthology, pages 115–116). Choose two paragraphs and list all the nouns in those paragraphs. Then form a plural for each noun that you listed.

Apply It

Write a five-sentence paragraph and use a variety of words that form their plurals in different ways. Write a five-sentence paragraph that contains at least three possessive nouns.

Keep at It

Complete Line Master 13 (available from your teacher) to support your understanding of how to pluralize nouns.

Pronouns

Before You Start

A pronoun is a word that replaces a noun. There are two different kinds of pronouns. Personal pronouns refer to a specific person or thing. Indefinite pronouns do not refer to someone or something specific.

PERSONAL PRONOUNS

A personal pronoun refers to a specific person or thing.

There are three forms of personal pronouns: subject pronoun (who is doing the action), object pronoun (the person to whom the action is being done), and possessive pronouns (to show ownership).

Singular

Subject	Object	Possessive
I	me	my, mine
you	you	your, yours
he, she, it	him, her, it	his, her, hers, its

Plural

Subject	Object	Possessive
we	us	our, ours
you	you	your, yours
they	them	their, theirs

Using personal pronouns makes writing more interesting and prevents repetition. Read Model 1. What do you notice?

Model 1

John is my neighbour. John works at Benson's Auto fixing cars. John really knows how to tell what's wrong with your car. John can tell what's working well or what needs repair just by listening to the sound of your engine. I respect John for his ability.

In Model 2, the noun John is replaced twice with "he." How does the change make the paragraph sound different?

Model 2

John is my neighbour. He works at Benson's Auto fixing cars. John really knows how to tell what's wrong with your car. He can tell what's working well or what needs repair just by listening to the sound of your engine. I respect John for his ability.

INDEFINITE PRONOUNS

An indefinite pronoun doesn't refer to a specific person or thing.

These indefinite pronouns are singular. Use them with singular forms of verbs, and with the singular possessive pronouns 'his', 'her', and 'its.'

another	anything	everybody	neither
anybody	each	everyone	nobody
somebody	anyone	either	everything
no one	someone		

Each of the jobs has its rewards.
Everyone cast his or her ballot.

These indefinite pronouns are plural. Use them with plural forms of verbs, and with the plural possessive pronouns 'their' and 'theirs.'

| both | few | many | several |

Many of the viewers expressed their opinions.
Several voiced their anger.

These indefinite pronouns can be singular or plural. If they refer to one thing, they are singular. If they refer to more than one thing, they are plural.

| all | any | most | none | some |

None of the actors knew their lines.
None of the furniture is in its appropriate place.
Most of the job is easy.
Most of the materials are available.

Act on It

Read "Rude Awakenings" (Anthology, pages 78–81). List the nouns and pronouns in the first five paragraphs. Discuss how they were used. Try using pronouns in place of nouns. Is the meaning still clear? Discuss where the writer used nouns rather than pronouns.

Apply It

Create a writing sample by describing your best friend. Use the person's name and no pronouns. Give the sample to a partner and have your partner decide where pronouns should replace nouns. Do you agree? Discuss it.

Keep at It

Write a letter of complaint about how a customer treated you at work. Make sure you have used nouns and pronouns appropriately. Share the letter of complaint with a partner.

Verbs

Before You Start

Every sentence has a verb. There are two kinds of verbs. A verb can be an action word that tells that something is, did, or will happen. A verb can also be a word that describes a state of being. The following are some examples of verbs.

Action words

cried *(The baby cried.)*
meet *(Kai will meet us at the coffee shop.)*
answers *(She answers the phone at the veterinary clinic.)*

State-of-being words

is *(My brother is a lawyer.)*
seems *(She seems ill.)*

Act on It

Read "Man in Action" (Anthology, pages 228-231). Find and list at least 10 verbs. Identify whether they are action verbs or state-of-being verbs. Share your list with a partner.

Apply It

Read an article in the newspaper. Read it a second time, making note of the verbs that the writer used. Write a personal response to the article. Explain whether you think the writer made good verb choices, how the verbs made you feel as you read, and what verbs you might have used instead. Share your response with a partner.

Keep at It

Choose a writing piece that you have completed previously. Underline the verbs. Identify whether they are state-of-being verbs or action verbs. Change the state-of-being verbs and make them action verbs. How does this change your writing piece?

Adjectives

Before You Start

There are several kinds of words that modify, or change, other words. We call these modifiers. One kind of modifier is an adjective. Adjectives are most often used to describe nouns, and are used in three different ways. Adjectives can show:

- which one

  this, that *(this street, that page)*

- what kind

  yellow, broken *(yellow flowers, broken photocopier)*

- how many or how much

  six, thirty, all *(six apples, thirty kilometres, all families)*

Most adjectives come before the word they are changing. A predicate adjective comes after a state-of-being verb, and modifies the subject of a sentence.

popular *(Soccer is popular all over the world.)*

Just as there are proper nouns, there are also proper adjectives.

Greek, English *(Greek food, English toffee)*

The adjectives 'a,' 'an,' and 'the' are called articles.

The job is perfect for me.

Act on It

Read "Bittersweet Memories of a Rock Hero" (Anthology, pages 138-140). Find and list at least 10 adjectives. Identify one that is an article, and at least two that tell 'which one', two that tell 'which kind', and two that tell 'how many'. Find one proper adjective in the selection.

Apply It

Write a description of an event that you really enjoyed. Write at least three paragraphs to describe it and make it as vivid to the reader as it is in your mind. Include adjectives, remembering the rules for using them.

Keep at It

Choose an ad from a magazine. Rewrite it, making the ad more vivid by using a variety of descriptive adjectives.

Adverbs

Before You Start

Like adjectives, adverbs are modifiers. They add to the meaning of a word. An adverb tells how, when, where, or to what degree. Adverbs often come after verbs, to give more specific information about the verb.

quickly *(The tickets sold quickly.)*
tomorrow *(Mei Lin gets here tomorrow.)*
miserably *(He failed miserably.)*

The word 'very' is an adverb added to a modifier to further enhance the meaning of a verb.

The girl danced well.
The girl danced very well.

Many adverbs are formed from adjectives by adding 'ly' to the end of the word.

Adjective	**Adverb**
soft	softly
loud	loudly

There are exceptions, of course. The following are all adverbs that don't use 'ly'.

too   so   quite   rather   somewhat

The usage of the words 'good' and 'well' is often confused. 'Good', an adjective, is always used to modify a noun.

Latoya is my good friend.

'Good' never modifies a verb, and almost never comes at the end of a sentence.

He did good. — incorrect
He did well. — correct

'Well' is usually an adverb, but can be an adjective. It almost always comes after a verb, or at the end of a sentence.

He did well in his exams.
She does not feel well.

Act on It

Read "Alone on the Ocean" (Anthology, pages 111–114). List 10 adverbs in your notebook. For each, explain, using the rules noted here, how you know it is an adverb. State beside each adverb the word that it modifies in the text.

Apply It

If you wrote descriptive paragraphs for the activity on adjectives (page 198), rewrite it and make it more vivid by adding adverbs to modify some of the verbs. If you did not write those paragraphs, write a description of an event that you really enjoyed. Write at least three paragraphs to describe that event and make it as vivid to the reader as it is in your mind. Include adjectives and adverbs.

Keep at It

Write a dialogue. Decide on a humorous, anxious, angry, or frightened tone. Use an adverb after each verb to describe how the person speaks. Be sure your adverb choice supports the tone you have chosen.

Conjunctions and Prepositions

Before You Start

Conjunctions and prepositions are connective words: they connect words, phrases, and paragraphs. When you add conjunctions and prepositions to your writing, you make your writing clear, logical, and interesting to the reader.

COORDINATING CONJUNCTIONS

The most familiar conjunctions are coordinating conjunctions — 'and', 'but', 'or', 'yet', 'nor', 'so'. They show how two sentences work together. Use these words to join sentences and to show how they are related.

Shani and Mary will help me.
The job was well paying but stressful.
It's payday, so I'm going right to the bank with my cheque.

PAIRS OF CONJUNCTIONS

Some conjunctions work in pairs.

either/or, neither/nor, both/and, not only/but also, whether/or

Either she leaves the party, or I leave.
Not only is the office tiny, but the building is old and dark.
I wasn't sure whether to take the subway or walk.

SUBORDINATE CONJUNCTIONS

Subordinate conjunctions connect two clauses together. They show that one clause is more important than the other. Here are some commonly used subordinate conjunctions:

after	before	in order that	that	whenever
although	but that	lest	though	where
whereas	if	how	why	while
whether	unless	though	because	as
when	once	since	even though	than

I came to work this morning although I was here until 11:00 last night.
He walks faster than I do.
The union achieved the settlement because they had a lot of support.

PREPOSITIONS

Prepositions are also connective words. Along with joining words or groups of words, they show relationships between things.

Some prepositions show:

- general relationships

  about, for, from, like, of, with

  She told me about her new job.

- location relationships

  against, in, near, on, through

  I parked my car near the sign.

- time relationships

  before, during, since, until, at

  I worked until noon.

Act On It

Read the first two paragraphs of "Incident Report" (Anthology, pages 176-177). List in your notebook all the prepositions included. Identify whether they show a time, location, or general relationship.

Apply It

With a partner, use the examples of prepositions given above to write instructions to get from one place to another. Use as many prepositions as you can.

Keep at It

Write a three-paragraph, one-page essay that describes a working experience you have had or would like to have. Choose three subordinate conjunctions and use one in each paragraph. Ask another student to read your essay and to underline the subordinate conjuctions. Did you use them correctly?

SENTENCES
Sentence Structures

Before You Start

A sentence has two basic parts: the subject and the predicate. The subject is the person, place, or thing that the sentence is about. The predicate contains a verb, and says, tells, or asks something about the subject.

To create interesting writing, you need to use different sentence structures. A paragraph made up of only simple sentences is choppy and doesn't read smoothly. A paragraph made up of many complex sentences can be hard to follow.

SIMPLE SENTENCES

A simple sentence has only two basic parts, subject and predicate.

subject — *The dog barked.* — predicate

Both parts of a sentence can be compound, or have more than one part.

This sentence has a compound subject:

compound subject — *The dog and cat fought.*

This sentence has a compound predicate:

The dog barked and yowled. — compound predicate

COMPOUND SENTENCES

A compound sentence links together two simple sentences with words such as 'and' or 'but', sometimes followed by a comma. A semicolon can also link two sentences.

Time is ticking away, and I'm accomplishing nothing.

The lake is cold but the air is warm.

It's time to go; we've overstayed our welcome.

COMPLEX SENTENCES

Clauses are groups of words that have both a subject and a predicate. Clauses that can stand alone are called independent clauses, or sentences. Clauses that can't stand alone are called dependent clauses. They need to be linked to a sentence, because by themselves they don't provide all the information the reader needs.

If you group together one or more main clauses and one or more subordinate clauses, you create a complex sentence.

Taylor cried whenever I left.
Ravi started his new job on Tuesday, because Monday was a statutory holiday.
Although I was sorry that she was sick, I was happy to buy her ticket to the concert.

Act on It

Read the first paragraph of "A Journey to the Woods" (Anthology, pages 108–110). Identify one simple sentence, one compound sentence, and one complex sentence. Write the complex sentence in your notebook. Identify the subject, predicate, main clause, subordinate clause, and linking word.

Apply It

Write a paragraph on any topic you choose, using as many different kinds of sentences as possible. For more information on writing paragraphs, see How to Write a Paragraph, pages 58-61.

Trade paragraphs within a group of three or four classmates. Invite each group member to identify a simple sentence, a compound sentence, and a complex sentence from another member's paragraph.

Keep at It

Choose a piece of writing you have previously completed. Improve your writing by editing your sentences so that you have included a variety of sentence structures.

Common Sentence Errors

Before You Start

The most common sentence errors are the sentence fragment and the comma splice. Once you can identify them, you can fix them in your own writing. As you edit or peer edit your work, look at each place you have included a comma. Then check to see if you have made a comma splice error.

A comma splice error occurs when two statements are joined together incorrectly by a comma, and should instead be two separate sentences, or should be linked using 'and', 'but', 'because', or 'when'.

I want to visit Rahim, he is my best friend. — incorrect; comma splice error

I want to visit Rahim because he is my best friend. — correct

I want to visit Rahim. He is my best friend. — correct, but overly simple and not very interesting

A sentence fragment error is a subordinate clause with no main clause to support it. It represents an incomplete thought. If you read the fragment, it will sound incomplete.

When I returned home. — sentence fragment error

When I returned home, I had a shower. — correct

I was exhausted when I returned home. — correct

Act on It

Look at a piece of writing that you have completed recently. Check for any comma splice or sentence fragment errors. If you find any, write the incorrect sentence in your notebook, then write the correct sentence.

Apply It

Find a partner to work with. Each of you should write a paragraph about a topic of your choice. Include one sentence fragment error and one comma splice error. Then trade paragraphs, and find and correct the errors included.

Keep at It

Turn to page 9 in your anthology ("Teach Me the Ways of the Sacred Circle"). Read Elaine's second speech on the page. Identify the sentence fragments in her speech. Discuss with your classmates why the playwright used sentence fragments. Look at some recent examples of your own writing. Did you use sentence fragments anywhere with a specific purpose? Explain.

PUNCTUATION
Ending a Sentence

Before You Start

All punctuation marks are signposts in writing that help readers know how to read a passage. Punctuation tells a reader when to pause and for how long, when to stop, when to consider a question, and when to feel strongly.

There are several punctuation marks that you can use to end a sentence. They include a period (.), a question mark (?), and an exclamation mark (!). Ending punctuation should only be used with a complete sentence (see Common Sentence Errors, page 205).

THE PERIOD

A period ends a sentence that makes a statement. When you are stating a fact, writing an opinion, or making a statement that has no great emotion attached to it, use a period. Most sentences end with a period.

I ate lunch.
Twenty-seven people boarded the aircraft.
I think I left my key on the table.

When you are using quotation marks, the period goes inside the end quotation mark.

"I'll meet you for lunch at 12:15."

Periods are not used to end titles, even if the title is a sentence.

A Fine Balance
Fall on Your Knees

THE QUESTION MARK

A question mark at the end of a sentence shows that the writer is asking for information.

Who is the author?
Did Janine leave yet?

When you are using quotation marks, the question mark goes inside the end quotation mark if the question is part of the quotation.

"Is Devon joining us tonight?"

Do use a question mark in a title if the title is a question.

Who's Afraid of Virginia Woolf?

THE EXCLAMATION POINT

An exclamation point is used to show strong feelings or emotions. Do not overuse exclamation points in your writing, or your reader won't know which information is really meant to show strong emotion.

"I don't believe it!" he cried.
She was highly insulted!

When you are using quotation marks, the exclamation point goes inside the end quotation mark if the exclamation is part of the quotation.

"Stop that man!" the group shouted.

Act on It

Find a passage from the anthology that includes dialogue. Using punctuation and descriptive language, change the tone, or feeling, of the dialogue to the opposite of what it was.

Apply It

Write a short dialogue that involves a conversation in which the tone changes from pleasant to angry. Use punctuation to set the tone.

Keep at It

Using a newspaper account of an incident, change the entire article into a dialogue. Be sure to use appropriate vocabulary and punctuation to reflect the tone of the article.

The Comma

Before You Start

The punctuation mark that people use most often in their writing is a comma (,). When it is used the right way, the comma helps readers understand what they are reading. A comma creates a short pause before a word or group of words. Commas can introduce information, separate ideas, or group ideas and information.

A comma can:

- introduce

  John, my new boss, is an expert drywaller.

- introduce a question that a writer has

  Should I tell Mr. Akande now, or wait until later when he's in a better mood?

- introduce the exact words that someone is saying

  Mahmood clearly said to me, "We need to place that order now."

- separate the name of a person to whom you are speaking

  Cheego, will you please speak more clearly?

- separate independent parts of a sentence that are joined by 'and', 'but', 'yet', 'neither', 'nor', or 'or'

  She was very late, but she brought all of the food.

- separate a group of descriptive words

  The red Mustang was old, rusty, unpredictable, and on its last legs.

- separate dates and places

  He left on May 10, 2002, to go to Winnipeg, Manitoba for an interview.

- help make the meaning of a sentence clear by marking added information

  My employer, the owner of a new company which has just moved to town, is now hiring.

Act On It

Write the following sentence in a journal or notebook. Place commas wherever you think they need to be to make the sentence make sense.

That that is is that that is not is not.

Apply It

Imagine you are the main witness to a traffic accident. Write a report for a police officer that outlines, clearly, what you saw. Make sure that you have used the right punctuation.

Keep at It

Keep working on your use of commas. Ask your teacher for Line Master 14 for practice.

Other Punctuation

> Before You Start

When you read, you come across different punctuation marks. The following is an explanation of the use of some of them, including the colon, semicolon, parentheses, dash, hyphen, and the apostrophe.

THE COLON

The colon has several different uses.

Use a colon:

- when you give a list after the words *as follows*

    The items you will need are as follows:

    2 tin cans
    a ball of string
    a pair of scissors
    tape

- before a quotation

    The poster read: "The Army: there's no life like it."

- in a very formal letter (for example, to a judge or a political leader), after the greeting

    Your Honour:

- to introduce an explanation

    The women by the pool were wearing the newest sunwear: long, light skirts made of nearly transparent Indian cotton, and loose-fitting shirts with long sleeves in a matching fabric.

THE SEMICOLON

Semicolons create long pauses in your writing.

Use a semicolon:

- between two sentences which present related ideas

    The pilot spoke to the passengers; he indicated that there was a problem.

- to separate items in a list that contains other punctuation

    Shairose had many job offers to choose from: The Burger Joint, which gave her 40 hours a week but low pay; the drycleaner's, which offered higher wages but fewer hours; and the convenience store, which gave her a flexible schedule.

PARENTHESES

Parentheses are used to enclose material which is not of major importance to the rest of a sentence, but which offers extra information.

During my trip to Calgary (that's the trip I won in the lottery!), I became very sick.

THE DASH

A dash helps draw attention to key ideas in a sentence.

Use a dash

- to separate an explanation from the rest of a sentence

    The Boston Marathon — an annual event that involves thousands of runners from all over the world — is a grueling race even for those who are well trained.

- to separate a series of words from a summary that will follow

    Cooks, bartenders, wait staff, bussers, dishwashers — these are the positions for which the restaurant is hiring.

- to show a sudden change of tone

    Cyril was exquisite — exquisitely boring.

THE HYPHEN

The hyphen has a variety of uses and a variety of exceptions to the rules.

Use a hyphen:

- after the word 'self' and the prefix 'ex' at the beginning of a word

    self-defence   self-interest   self-reliant   ex-fighter   ex-boyfriend

- to help distinguish the meaning of a word that might be confused with another word

    re-cover, not recover
    (re-cover a chair with new fabric rather than recover something lost)
    re-creation, not recreation
    (to create again rather than to have leisure time)

- to avoid using two e's or two o's together in a word

    co-operate   re-enter   re-examine   co-ordinate

Spelling with Hyphens

Do not hyphenate:
- the following compound words

    myself, yourself, himself

- or these compound words

altogether	*anyone*	*basketball*	*baseball*	*bathroom*
bookmark	*cannot*	*daylight*	*farmhouse*	*fireproof*
forehead	*foresee*	*framework*	*grapefruit*	*handbag*
handwriting	*homework*	*notebook*	*nowadays*	*oneself*
outdoors	*overcharge*	*pillowcase*	*secondhand*	*semicolon*
snowstorm	*today*	*tomorrow*	*tonight*	

- a pronoun or adverb ending with body, thing, where

    anybody, somewhere, something

- points of a compass

    northwest, southeast

- a two-part word that includes an 'ly' adverb and comes before a noun to describe it

    smartly dressed man

These are always separate words:

all right	*good night*	*high school*	*post office*
per cent	*ranch house*	*school year*	*school bus* *will power*

Always hyphenate:
- the following words:

    self-respect   good-bye   re-enter   pin-up

- any two-part word that comes before a noun and is used to describe it

high-strung	*so-called*	*good-bye*	*de-ice*
old-fashioned	*well-bred*	*left-handed*	*first-class*

Do not hyphenate an adjective formed by adding "like" to a one-syllable noun; do hyphenate if the noun has more than one syllable.

childlike   *doglike*   *business-like*   *tiger-like*

If you are unsure whether to hyphenate a word, look it up in the dictionary. If it is hyphenated, it should appear that way in the dictionary. If it is all one word, it should appear so in the dictionary. If it does not appear in the dictionary, write it as two separate words.

THE APOSTROPHE

An apostrophe is used to show possession, or is used in contractions to show that letters are being left out.

Possession

Use an apostrophe before the letter 's' to show possession for singular nouns or for plural nouns that don't end in 's.'

Akiko's teapot
the dog's ear
women's books
people's choice

Use an apostrophe to show possession for nouns that already end in 's.'

employees' parking spaces
bus' tail lights

Use an apostrophe before the letter 's' to show possession for indefinite pronouns.

everyone's right
no one's responsibility

Contractions

Use an apostrophe to show that a letter has been removed to create a contraction.

can not — can't   *do not — don't*   *they are — they're*

Use an apostrophe to show omission of numbers in a date.

2002 — '02

Act on It

Look through the anthology and find several selections where apostrophes have been used. List five examples in your notebook, and describe what kind of apostrophe it is.

Apply It

Errors in punctuation often happen because writers forget that punctuation helps readers make sense of text. With a partner, look at the punctuation rules noted in this section. Identify mechanical errors that you think you make, or punctuation marks that you don't use correctly yet. Make a plan to remember the correct way to use them.

Keep at It

Review the rules about hyphenation. Make a list of words that might cause you difficulty when you are trying to decide whether or not to hyphenate. Check them in the dictionary and share the correct spelling with the class.

Connecting Words

> ### Before You Start

One way to make your writing more interesting is to use a variety of sentences, including compound and complex sentences. Connecting words can help create these kinds of sentences. Connecting words link the ideas in various parts of a piece of writing by showing how those ideas relate.

Use connecting words within sentences.

Lots of great bands are playing at the festival, for example, Kittie, Peaches, and Dog Star.

Use connecting words between paragraphs.

. . . the law needs to change.

On the other hand, there are also reasons to think carefully before we make changes to this law.

Here are some connecting words and the relationships they show. You will notice that some of the connecting words are adverbs.

Use a connecting word:

- to list, add, introduce, or conclude

  to begin with, for a start, in the first place, first, second, third, and, also, for one thing, in addition, finally, lastly, in conclusion

  In conclusion, I'd like to thank you all for coming today.

- to reinforce

  clearly, furthermore, moreover, besides, above all

  Clearly, we have to do something to help the homeless.

- to elaborate

  for example, for instance, to illustrate, such as, namely, in other words, that is

  This jacket can be made in several fabrics, for example, denim, corduroy, or twill.

- **to show similarity**

  similarly, likewise

  Jamal seems to do very well in languages. Similarly, his twin brother enjoys learning languages.

- **to show contrast**

  instead, on the contrary, however, in spite of, on the other hand, yet, but, conversely, in contrast

  Jana loves to play hockey, but she doesn't love the early-morning practices.

- **to show cause and effect**

  thus, therefore, consequently, for this reason, because, since, accordingly, as a result, in order that, hence, so

  The winter has been unusually warm and dry. As a result, farmers are worried about the impact of the weather on their crops.

- **to concede**

  although, though, still, nevertheless, anyway, however, even though, even if, to be sure, granted that, whereas

  Although the car is old, it has great potential.

- **to locate**

  above, below, close by, nearby, next to, inside, opposite, within, without, further along

  The photocopier is next to the printer in the room at the end of the hall.

Act on It

Write a paragraph which describes how to make your favourite sandwich. Use appropriate connecting words to help move the reader from step to step.

Apply It

Choose and read an editorial from a newspaper. Try to find cause and effect connecting words. If they are not present in the writing, insert them where causes and effects are described. Share your changes with a partner. Which cause and effect words enhance the case the author is trying to make?

Keep at It

With a group, choose a school policy that you think needs to change. Write a paragraph that outlines the current policy and describes how changes would be beneficial to students. Include appropriate connecting words.

Direct and Indirect Speech

Before You Start

In your writing, you may want to tell, repeat, or describe the words of a character or person. To do this, you need to know how to write direct and indirect speech.

DIRECT SPEECH

Direct speech refers to the exact words that a speaker says. Place the speaker's words within quotation marks:

The ambulance driver shouted, "I need help, now!"

When you are writing direct speech, begin a new paragraph for each new speaker. This helps the reader to know that the speakers are changing.

"Hi," said Shawn.
"Hello, Shawn," replied Anita.
"It's been years since we last met," commented Shawn.
"You're right," responded Anita.
"It's been at least five years."
"You must be right, Shawn."

If a quotation is divided by a reference to the speaker, use two sets of quotation marks, one set on either side of the reference to the speaker.

Here, the quotation is divided into two separate sentences.

"I'm so sorry," he answered. "I didn't hear what you said."

Here, the quotation continues the original sentence, so there is no capital on 'if'.

"It's hard to tell," she continued, "if I'm doing the right thing."

INDIRECT SPEECH

Indirect speech refers to reporting the words that someone said. The words may or may not be exact.

The ambulance driver said that he needed help right away.

Quotation marks are not needed for indirect speech.

CREATING VIVID DIALOGUE

When you write direct speech or dialogues, you need to show what is said and how it is said. Punctuation and effective word choices can help you write dialogue that comes alive on the page.

Use punctuation to show how words are spoken.

"Help!" yelled Parker.
"Help?" asked Parker. "Is help what you need?"

Instead of using the word 'said', use active verbs and adverbs to further describe how a character feels while he or she is speaking.

"Help!" yelled Parker frantically.

Here is a list of words to replace 'said'.

commented	quipped	squeaked	argued	told
retorted	reminded	pursued	denied	exclaimed
supported	questioned	directed	demanded	asked
yelled	blurted	ordered	snorted	provided
cried	stammered	proclaimed	replied	shouted
uttered	roared	summoned	solicited	requested
interrupted	spoke	denounced	added	begged

Here is a list of adverbs that help add feeling to a verb.

smugly	politely	determinedly	quietly	worriedly
tersely	sheepishly	forcefully	meekly	boastfully
wryly	suspiciously	arrogantly	rudely	clearly
passionately	cruelly	happily	boisterously	forgivingly

Act on It

Read "Harriet's Daughter" in the anthology (pages 24–29). Identify four examples of direct speech, then rewrite them in indirect speech.

Apply It

Create a 10-line dialogue about a girl asking a boy out on a date. Before you begin, outline the character traits of the boy and the girl. The personalities and feelings of the two characters should be clearly evident in the words and punctuation you use.

Keep at It

Choose a piece of text in the newspaper that describes an incident (you might consider using an accident report or even an obituary). Using the facts of the text, create a dialogue between two of the people named.

USING LANGUAGE
Synonyms

Before You Start

One of the best ways to improve your writing is to vary the words you choose. If you want to find different words that mean the same thing, called synonyms, you can use a thesaurus. A thesaurus is a book containing lists of synonyms. It gives you a supply of words to use in your writing. You may find a thesaurus helpful if the word you have chosen doesn't quite say what you want it to say.

To use a thesaurus, look up the word that you want to replace. Then read the list of other words that have the same meaning. Sometimes the meaning is exactly the same; other times, the words have a different feel or strength (see How to Understand Connotations of Words, pages 27–29).

This paragraph shows the repeated use of the word 'dislike'.

I dislike the way you treat me. I dislike the attitude you have about your work. Furthermore, I dislike the rude way in which you speak to customers.

In this paragraph, synonyms are used to replace the word 'dislike'.

I dislike the way you treat me. I disapprove of the attitude you have toward your work. I object to the rude way in which you speak to customers.

Act On It

Look up the word 'dislike' in a thesaurus. List the words you find there, then experiment with rewriting the model using various words in place of 'dislike'. Which version do you like best? Why?

Apply It

Choose a piece of writing that you have completed in the past. Using a thesaurus, rewrite your writing piece by using synonyms for some of the words. Be careful not to change the meaning of the passage.

Keep at It

With a partner, choose a topic. Taking turns so that you write every other sentence, write 10 sentences in total about the topic. When you are done, find synonyms to change one another's vocabulary. Do this several times until you are both satisfied that the vocabulary in your writing piece is the best it can be.

Antonyms

Before You Start

Antonyms are pairs of words that are opposite in meaning. When you are looking for the antonym of a word, be sure that it is the true opposite of the word.

Here are some antonyms

good/bad	up/down	liberal/conservative
success/failure	question/answer	competent/incompetent
superior/inferior	agree/disagree	employee/employer
true/false	dead/alive	whole/broken
love/hate		

You can make the exact opposite of a word by adding a prefix that means 'not', such as 'un', 'in', 'im', or 'dis'.

clear/unclear	professional/unprofessional	complete/incomplete
perfect/imperfect	service/disservice	

Act on It

Choose two paragraphs from "Don't Give Up on the Media" (Anthology, pages 122–123). Find antonyms for five words in the selection you chose, then list the words and their antonyms in your notebook.

Apply It

For fun, change the tone of the selection you chose above. Replace the words you chose from the selection with the antonym you found for each one. Do the same with a short writing piece of your own.

Keep at It

Work with a partner. Each of you should write a four-sentence, descriptive paragraph. Trade paragraphs and use antonyms to change the tone of each piece of writing.

Homonyms

Before You Start

The most difficult thing about the English language is understanding that two or more words may sound the same, but be spelled differently and have completely different meanings. These words are called homonyms. Here is one common example of homonyms at work.

They're going to have the party at the restaurant over **there**, because they don't want **their** house destroyed.

Why do all three words sound the same but have different spellings and meanings?

- **They're** is the contraction of the two words 'they' and 'are'.
- **There** is a directional word indicating a specific place.
- **Their** is a plural possessive pronoun used to show ownership.

Here is a list of some commonly used homonyms.

aye – eye	heal – heel	pray – prey
air – heir	him – hymn	principal – principle
borough – burro – burrow	its –it's	rain – reign
brake – break	flocks – phlox	their – there – they're
dear – deer	for – fore – four	time – thyme
dew – do	mail – male	to – too – two
cellar – seller	missed – mist	wait – weight
cite – sight – site	one – won	way – weigh
fair – fare	pail – pale	weak – week
grate – great	peace – piece	you'll – yule
hair – hare	plain – plane	

Act on It

In a "think-pair-share" activity, discuss each grouping of words and explain how they are different in meaning. Can you add any other word groupings to the list on this page? Add them to your notebook.

Apply It

Of all the homonyms listed, indicate the ones that you think are used most often. Try to come up with some rules to help you remember correct usage. Record the rules in your notebook.

Keep at It

In a group, choose a topic, then write a paragraph that uses as many homonyms as possible. Each group member takes a turn writing a sentence that includes a pair of homonymns. Write eight to 10 sentences. Share your paragraph with the class. Have you used the homonyms correctly?

Spelling Rules

Before You Start

English is a language with nearly as many exceptions to its spelling rules as there are spelling rules. Here you'll find a few rules which, along with the other information in this grammar clinic, will help you with your spelling when you write.

DOUBLING A FINAL CONSONANT

Double the final consonant when you add a vowel suffix (er, est) to a word that ends in a single vowel followed by a single consonant (for example, big), and that is one syllable or has the accent on the last syllable (for example, occur). Here are some examples.

stop	+	ed	=	stopped
stop	+	ing	=	stopping
big	+	er	=	bigger
big	+	est	=	biggest
wit	+	y	=	witty
begin	+	er	=	beginner
begin	+	ing	=	beginning
occur	+	ed	=	occurred
occur	+	ing	=	occurring

DROPPING FINAL E

When adding a suffix drop the final 'e' on words that end with a silent 'e.' Here are some examples.

dare	+	ing	=	daring
arrange	+	ing	=	arranging
admire	+	ation	=	admiration
fame	+	ous	=	famous
guide	+	ance	=	guidance

WORDS WITH 'EI' AND 'IE'

This poem might help you remember where to place 'i' and 'e' in a word

'I' before 'e' except after 'c'.
Or when sounded like 'a'
As in neighbour and weigh.

- so, 'i' before 'e':

  achieve   *besiege*   *cashier*   *chief*   *grief*
  mischievous *piece*   *relieve*

- except after 'c':

  ceiling   *conceive*   *deceit*   *receipt*

- sounded like 'a':

  freight   *neighbour*   *reign*   *vein*   *weight*

Some exceptions to the rules in the poem are these words.

weird, height, leisure, foreign, counterfeit, forfeit, heifer, sleight, species

Also when 'c' is pronounced 'sh', 'c' is followed by 'ie'

ancient, conscience, efficient, proficient, sufficient

Act on It

In a small group, prepare a spelling test for the class. Present the test, then mark it. Let the other students have time to correct their answers, then have them take the test again.

Apply It

In a small group, choose one of the spelling rules here. Create an activity to teach the rule to the class and help people remember it.

Keep at It

In a small group, create rap lyrics that address and help people remember a spelling rule of the group's choice.

Index

A
abbreviations, classified ads, 178, 179
action words, 76–77
active voice, 133, 196
addresses
    e-mail, 89
    verbal. *See* oral summaries; presentations
    Web site. *See* URL
adjectives, 197–198, 199
    (*See also* predicate adjectives)
adverbs, 199–200
advertisement(s)(*See also* classified ads; commercials; display ads; image ads; promotional ads)
    analyzing, 174–176
    creating, 176–178
    defined, 174
    exercises, 179
    hidden messages in, 186
    types of, 174
    tips, 176
affixes, 4, 124, 125
alliteration, 21, 176
antagonist, 31
antonyms, 224
apostrophe, 214
articles (magazines/newspapers), 156
articles (parts of speech), 197
audience (*See also* target audience)
    appropriate language, 133
    media, 147, 148, 164, 165, 171
    response, manipulating, 172, 176, 184, 186
    speaker's, 136–137
    writer's, 50, 132, 133
audiotape, interview, 142

B
bar graph, 43, 45
base word. *See* root word
bias
    defined, 170
    exercises, 173
    identifying, 170–173
    model, 172–173
    types of, 170
bias by commission, 170
bias by omission, 170
bias in a statement, 170
block (letter) style, 85
body copy, display ad, 175, 176
body language, 102, 142, 172, 175, 185 (*See also* eye contact; facial expressions; gestures, speaker's)
books, citing as source, 55

C
camera angles, 172, 184, 186
caption, 43, 155
career-objective statement, 77
career, researching, 54
    (*See also* résumé(s))
cause/effect diagrams, 110
cause and effect organizer, 105, 110
character(s)
    conflict, 31–32, 37–50
    element of narrative, 31
    narrative point of view, 32
    television portrayal of, 171
character sketch, 37–41
charts, 7, 42 (*See also* chronology chart; compare/contrast charts; sequence charts; skills charts; story chart)
chronological résumé, 76, 80
chronology charts, 110
circle graph, 43, 46
citing sources, 55, 151
classified ads, creating, 178–179
clauses, 204
closing sentence, 13
closings, formal letter, 70
colon, 211
columns (newspapers, magazines), 154
combination résumé, 76, 81
comma, 209–210
comma splice, 205
commercials, 174, 175, 186
common nouns, 191
common sentence errors, 205–206
compare/contrast charts, 110
comparisons, signal words, 110
complex sentences, 204
compound predicate, 203
compound sentences, 203
compound subject, 203
concluding paragraph, 7
concluding statement (paragraph), 59
conclusions diagrams, 111
conflict(s)
    character, 37, 38, 39
    element of narrative, 31
    fiction, 24
    models, 25–26
    types of, 31–32
conjunctions, 201–202
connecting words, 48, 63, 216–217, 218
connective words. *See* conjunctions; prepositions
connotative meaning, 27–29
content
    in analyzing for bias, 171
    revising for, 52
contractions, 214
coordinating conjunctions, 201
covering letter, résumé, 70, 71
    defined, 83
    exercises, 88
    format, 86, 87
    samples, 73, 87
    tips, 86
critical analysis
    literature, 33–36
    media, 148
    television program, 165–166
    in writing process, 53
cultural bias, 171–172
cutline, 43, 155
cuts (magazines, newspapers), 155

D
dash, 212
decisions (possible outcomes), organizer, 111
deck, 43, 154
dependent clauses, 204

Index

descriptive paragraph, 59, 60
design (*See also* layout)
    advertising, 176
    group work, 118–119
    magazines/newspapers, 155, 156, 157
    print, 8
diagram, 7, 43 (See also; conclusion diagrams; flow chart diagrams)
    character sketch, 38
dialogue, vivid, 220, 221
dictionaries, 129 (*See also* personal dictionary; thesaurus)
dictionary meaning, words, *27*
direct speech, 219
directly stated bias, 170
directly stated information, reading skill, 4
display ads, 154, 174, 175
    creating, 176–177
doubling final consonant, 227
drawing conclusions, organizer, 111
dropping final "e" (spelling), 227

E

editing, steps of, 52–53
    and personal style guide, 129–130
editorials, 154
"ei" and "ie" words, 228
e-mail address, 89
e-mail etiquette, 90
e-mail, writing and sending, 90
    exercises, 91
    job applications, 85, 89
    sample, 91
    tips, 91
ending punctuation, 207–208
errors (sentence), 205–206
exclamation point, 208
explicit (directly stated) bias, 170
expository paragraph, 59, 61
eye contact, 97, 142

F

facial expressions, speaker's, 102
features (magazines, newspapers), 154
figures, 7, 42
film
    citing as source, 55
    oral summary of, 107–108
first-person point of view, 32, 133
5 Ws and H, 162, 164
flow chart diagrams, 111
flow charts, 42
formal letters
    defined, 70
    elements of, 70
    steps, 70–71
    types of, 72–74
format
    choosing (written work), 50
    covering letter, 85, 87
    formal letters, 70
    group research, 118
    media, 147, 149
    personal dictionary, 122–123
    résumés, 78
    visual information, 42–45
functional résumé, 76, 79

G

gestures, speaker's, 102
"good" (correct usage), 199
grammar
    revising for, 53
    rules of, 190–228 (*See also* style guides)
graphic organizers, 105, 106–107, 110–112, 123
graphs, 7, 42
    types of, 43, 45–46
group discussions, summarizing, 110–112
group members, effective
    exercises, 116
    sample group, 115–116
    steps, 113–114
    tips, 114
group skills, 94, 95, 97, 113
group work, effective
    creating, 156
    exercises, 120
    sample, 120
    steps, 117–119
    tips, 119

H

hidden messages, advertising, 186
homonyms, 225–226
hyphen, 212–214

I

ideas
    generating, organizer, 110
    writing process, 51
image ads, 175
imagery, 21, 176
imperative verbs, 133
implicit (indirectly stated) bias, 170
indefinite pronouns, 194
independent clauses, 204
indirect speech, 220
indirectly stated bias, 170
indirectly stated information, reading skill, 5
informational interviews, 141, 143
informational text, oral summary, 105
instruction manuals, 99
instructions, oral, 98–100
Internet, citing as source, 55, 151
Internet searches, 54, 55, 56, 150
    exercises, 153
    models, 56, 152
    sources, 152
    steps, 150–151
    tips, 151–152
interpreting text, reading skill, 5
interviews, 141–143
introductory paragraph, 7

J

job advertisements, 83–84, 178
    (*See also* classified ads)
job applications by e-mail, 85, 89
job interviews, 141, 143
job-objective statement, 77
job searches, 55, 150, 152
jumplines, 155

Index

K
key words, 4, 102

L
language–choosing appropriate
    exercises, 135
    model, 134
    steps, 132–133
    tips, 133
language skills, 94–144
layout
    display ads, 176
    magazines, 155, 157
leads (articles), 156
letterhead template, résumés, 77
letters
    to editor, 155
    format, 85
    formal, 70–75
    covering, résumés, 70, 71, 83–88
line graph, 43, 46
linking words. *See* connecting words
listening
    exercises, 104
    sample speech, 103–104
    skills, 94, 95–96, 113, 119
    steps, 102–103
    tips, 103
literature
    elements of narrative, 30–32
    personal response to, 33

M
magazines
    citing as source, 55
    compared to newspapers, 155
    creating, steps, 156–157
    elements of, 154–155
    exercises, 158–159
    layout, 155, 157
main heading, 7 (*See also* subheading)
maps, 42, 45
media–analyzing
    audience, 147
    bias, 170–173
    influences on media creators, 146
    making connections, 148
    media formats, 147
media experience, organizer, 105, 106–107
media skills, 149
media techniques, 186
memory, oral summaries, 106
memory aids, listening, 103
message, in identifying bias, 172
metaphors, 21
modified block style, 85, 87
modifiers, 197 (*See also* adjectives; adverbs)
motivation, character, 37, 39, 138

N
narrative, elements of, 30, 31–32
narrative paragraph, 59, 60
narrative point of view, 32
negative bias, types of, 170
news reports. *See* radio news reports
newspapers
    citing as source, 55, 57
    compared to magazines, 155
    creating, steps, 156–157
    elements of, 154, 157
    layout, 155, 157
    model, 157
    wire services, 158
new words, 125, 126
news stories, 154
note-taking
    interviews, 142
    media experiences, 149, 166, 171
    for oral summaries, 105 (*See also* organizers)
    research, 55
    study cards, 9
    summarizing group discussions, 111
    while listening, 103
nouns, 191
    exercises, 192, 195
numbering visuals, 43

O
object pronouns, 193
online information, cautions about, 150, 151, 154
opinion papers, writing
    exercises, 66
    models, 63–65
    steps, 62–63
    tip, 62
opposites (words). *See* antonyms
oral instructions, following
    exercises, 100–101
    model, 99
    steps, 98–99
    tips, 99
oral summaries
    creating, 105–106
    defined, 105
    exercises, 108–109
    presenting, 106
    sample organizers, 106–108
    tips, 106
organizers, 106–108

P
pairs of conjunctions, 201
paper
    covering letter, 86
    résumé, 78
paragraph(s) (*See also* concluding paragraph; introductory paragraph)
    defined, 58
    exercises, 61
    summarizing, 13–15
    types of, 59
    writing, steps, 58–59
parentheses, 212
parts of speech, 190
    adjectives, 197
    adverbs, 199–200
    conjunctions, 201–202
    nouns, 192–192
    prepositions, 202
    pronouns, 193
    verbs, 196
passive voice, 133

period, 207
personal dictionary, 121–123
personal pronouns, 193–194
personal response, to literature, 33
personal style guide–creating
    exercises, 131
    model, 130
    steps, 128–129
    tips, 129
personification, 21
photographs, 42, 43
plural, nouns, 191–192
poetry, 16, 30
    analysis of, 20–23
point-form notes, 105, 106, 178
point of view, 32, 133, 171
positive bias, 170
possessive
    apostrophe, 213
    nouns, 192
    pronouns, 193
predicate, 203
predicate adjectives, 197
prefix, 4, 123, 124
prepositions, 202
presentations (*See also* oral summaries)
    effective, elements of, 136
    exercises, 140
    model, 138–139
    speaking skills, 96–97
    steps, 136–137
print, design features of, 8
promotional ads, 175
pronouns, 193
    exercises, 195
proper adjectives, 197
proper nouns, 191
prose analysis
    compared with poetry, 20
    exercises, 19
    models, 18–19
    tips, 17
publications, creating, 154–159
punctuation
    apostrophe, 214
    colon, 211

comma, 209–210
dash, 212
ending a sentence, 207–209
hyphen, 212–214
parentheses, 212
question mark, 207–208
semicolon, 211–212

Q
question mark, 207–208
questions, interview, 141

R
radio advertisers, 176
radio news report
    analyzing, 160–161
    creating, steps, 162
    exercises, 164
    models, 163–164
    tips, 161
reading strategies, 4–10
recognizing meaning, reading skills, 4
report writing
    exercises, 69
    model, 68–69
    steps, 67–68
    tips, 68
research
    defined, 54
    exercises, 37
    group, strategies, 117–120
    online. *See* Internet searches
    sample sources, 56–57
    steps, 54–55
    tips, 56
résumé(s)
    covering letter, 70, 71, 73, 83–88
    defined, 76
    exercises, 82
    steps, 76–77
    styles, 76, 79–81
revising written work, 52–53
rewriting, 53
root word(s), 4, 123, 124, 125

S
script, 180, 184 (*See also* storyboard)
search engines, 56, 151
searches, Internet, 55, 56, 150–153
semicolon, 211–212
sentence, ending (punctuation), 207–208
sentence errors, common, 205–206
sentence fragment, 205
sentence structure
    complex sentences, 204
    compound sentences, 203
    exercises, 204
    parts of, 203
    simple sentences, 203
    variety in, 52, 203
sequence charts, 110
short forms, classified ads, 178
showing order, 110 (*See also* signal words)
signal words, 111–112
similes, 21
simple sentences, 203
skills charts
    reading, 4–5
    résumé covering letter, 84–85
speaker's signals, 102–103
specialized vocabulary (*See also* personal dictionary)
    creating, 125
    exercises, 126–127
    neologism model, 126
    understanding, 124–125
sources
    citing, 55
    research, 54
speaking skills, 94, 95–97
spelling
    revising for, 53
    rules, 227–228
    with hyphens, 213–214
state-of-being (verb), 196
stereotypes, 170, 172
storyboards
    creating, steps, 180–181
    defined, 180
    exercises, 183

Index

model, 182–183
   tips, 181
structure, revising for, 52
study cards, 9 (*See also* index cards; note-taking)
style guides, 55, 129 (*See also* personal style guide)
subheadings, 7, 68
subject (of sentence), 203
subject pronoun, 193
subordinate conjunctions, 201–202
subtopics, 117, 118, 119
suffix, 4, 123, 124
summarizing discussions, graphic organizer, 110–112
summarizing paragraph, 13–15
symbolism, 21, 176
synonyms, 52, 122, 123, 222, 223

T
tables, 42, 44
target audience, 164, 171, 175
television program, how to view
   analyzing for bias, 171–172
   exercises, 168–169
   model, 166–168
   pros and cons, 169
   steps, 165–166
   tips, 166

text, elements of, 6–8
theme, element of narrative, 32
thesaurus, 52, 122, 222
third-person point of view, 32, 133
timelines, 110, 117
tone
   newscaster's, 171
   speaker's, 102, 162
   writer's, 17, 134
topic (written work)
   choosing, 50
   research, 54, 56
   versus theme, 32
topic sentence, 13, 58

U
URL (Uniform Resource Locator), 55, 56

V
values/ideas, evaluating, 24–56
verb forms, 133
verbal rehearsal, interviews, 98
verbs, 196, 220
video, citing as source, 55
video–creating
   basic elements, 184
   exercises, 187
   media techniques, 186
   steps, 184–185
   tips, 185
visual information, 42–47
visual organizer, 105, 106–107, 110–112
visualization, 98
vocabulary. *See* personal dictionary; specialized vocabulary)
voice (writing). *See* point of view; tone; verb forms

W
Web site(s)
   citing as source, 55, 151
   creating, 151
   evaluating, 153
"well" (correct usage), 199
white space, 176
word meaning, graphic organizer for, 123
words, vivid, 220
workplace, media in, 149
writer's guide. *See* personal style guide
writing process, 50–53
written instructions, 98

Acknowledgements

Every effort has been made to find and to acknowledge correctly the sources of the material reproduced in this book. The publisher welcomes any information that will enable it to rectify, in subsequent editions, any errors or omissions.

"My Cycling Life" by Steve Bauer. Reprinted by permission.

"All the Years of Her Life" by Morley Callaghan.

"The Berlin Wall Crashes Down" by Robert Darnton. From *Timetracks*, Nelson Thompson Learning, 1994.

"Foolish Hearts" from *Foolish Hearts*, courtesy of The Canadian Broadcasting Corporation/Société Radio-Canada.

"Chapter One/Odette" from *Counterpoint* by Marie Moser. Published by Clarke Irwin.

"Erosion" by E.J. Pratt. From *Black, Bright and Grey*, R.J. McMaster, ed. (Don Mills: Longmans Canada) 1969, University of Toronto Press.

"A teen's 'twisted' cry for help: Fictional story about avenging the bullies who tormented him lands 16-year-old in jail" by Aaron Sands. The Ottawa Citizen.

Résumés and Covering Letters adapted from *Good Job: A Young Person's Guide to Finding, Landing and Loving a Job* copyright © 2000 by Nancy Schaefer. Reprinted by permission of Stoddart Publishing Co. Limited.

"Learning about Electricity" from *ScienceWise 11*, published by Irwin Publishing Ltd. Reprinted with permission.

"Modelling Ads Mislead Youth" by Morning Star Trickey, from *Fresh Perspectives*.

"We stand up for advertising standards." Courtesy of Advertising Standards of Canada.

Visuals

page 14: MaXx Images/Dave Ryan, page 46, top: from Boom, Bust & Echo 200 copyright 1996 by David K. Foot. Reprinted by permission of Stoddart Publishing Co Limited., page 56: courtesy of Yahoo Canada, page 152: courtesy of monster.ca, page 157: courtesy of The *Chronicle-Journal*, Thunder Bay, Ontario (www.chroniclejournal.com), pages 182-183: John Martz